THE
HIGH HOLY DAYS

Popular History of Jewish Civilization

General Editor: Raphael Posner

THE
HIGH HOLY DAYS

Compiled by Naphtali Winter

LEON AMIEL PUBLISHER
New York–Paris

Published in the Western Hemisphere by
LEON AMIEL PUBLISHER
New York – Paris

ISBN 8148-0604-x

Printed in Israel

CONTENTS

INTRODUCTION

INTRODUCTION

The High Holy Days consist of two festivals: Rosh Ha-Shanah, New Year's Day, and Yom Kippur, the Day of Atonement. These two festivals are the most solemn days of the whole Jewish year and represent some of the most basic beliefs of the Jewish faith. On Rosh Ha-Shanah, God is acknowledged as King of the Universe, who sits in judgement over all His creatures, tempering justice with mercy. On the Day of Atonement, man seeks God through repentance and receives His pardon and full atonement.

These High Holy Days stress the spiritual bond between God and man. They have an extraordinary appeal and are anchored in Jewish tradition and imagination. In contrast to the levity and merriment with which the New Year is celebrated in many parts of the world by other nations the High Holy Days are marked by an atmosphere of sanctity. The acknowledgement of God's sovereignty and might instil a feeling of awe, and for this reason the two festivals are called the *Yamim Nora'im,* the Days of Awe. They are nevertheless also festivals and are celebrated with joy, but a joy of the spirit, when man may gain new insight and achieve a spiritual contentment far in excess of any material joy or happiness.

Unlike the other festivals of the Jewish calendar, both biblical and post-biblical, Rosh Ha-Shanah and Yom Kippur do not commemorate any historical event. It is this fact which lies behind a remarkable and even daring Midrash: the Ministering Angels entered the presence of the Holy One, blessed be He, and asked Him, "When is Rosh Ha-Shanah and when Yom Kippur?" to which He replied, "Do you then enquire of me? Let us both descend to the court on earth and enquire of them, as it is written, 'For it is a statute unto Israel'." Interpreted in mundane language, the Midrash emphasizes that the value of these solemn days is what we make of them.

Although the Days of Awe consist only of Rosh Ha-Shanah and Yom Kippur their impact is so powerful that both the preceding and intervening periods are affected. The complete month prior to Rosh Ha-Shanah, Elul, has become a period of preparation and the intervening days, the Ten Days of Penitence, are a bridge leading to the Day of Atonement. Yom Kippur is the spiritual climax but the period is concluded only on Hoshanah Rabbah, the last day of the Sukkot festival. The complete period, from the first day of Elul until the festival of Hoshanah Rabbah has thus become a period of fifty days.

The Festival Cycle

The Days of Awe are generally regarded as a festival unit in themselves. They should, however, also be regarded as an integral part of the annual festival cycle. This cycle begins with Pesaḥ (Passover) which represents the birth of the nation. Although freed from bondage, Israel did not become a nation until it received the Torah which made it unique among the peoples of the world. This stage is represented by Shavuot (Pentecost), which concludes the "national" festival unit, and is therefore also called "*Azeret*", a festival of termination. The "national" unit stresses the influence of God on the individual Jew and on the Jewish people. The following unit, the *Yamim Nora'im,* stress the striving of the individual and the nation, to reach God. The acknowledgement of God's providence and omnipresence (Rosh Ha-Shanah) leads to the realization of man's own inadequacy in the face of the divine (Yom Kippur). Paradoxically, this very realization of man's dependence on God permits man to climb to new heights by which he can be reconciled with God and reach absolute bliss. This final stage is represented by the festival of Sukkot, the "Feast of Joy", which is concluded by Shemini Azeret, the terminating festival, which completes the festival cycle.

"Yom Kippur Prayers" by Leopold Pilichowski.

1. ELUL

I Am My Beloved's And My Beloved Is Mine

Period of Preparation

Although well aware that even the best parable is unable to describe man's relationship with God, the rabbis still saw the parable as the most effective means available to the human understanding. In rabbinic tradition, therefore, God is frequently pictured as the King of Kings, and the reader is required to imagine how he would feel with regard to a "King of Flesh and Blood", and then to multiply that feeling infinitely with regard to God. Nowhere in the whole gamut of Jewish thought is this idea more pronounced than with regard to the High Holy Days. The sages see these days as constituting a "palace in time"; an invitation to a temporal royal palace demands adequate preparation from the lucky guest, how much more so a visit to the palace of the King of Kings, Almighty God.

The vestibule to this palace is the month of Elul, which is to be utilized for self-preparation for the most important occasion of man's spiritual year — Rosh Ha-Shanah and Yom Kippur.

The sages pointed out that its Hebrew letters are an acrostic *The Shofar* for the verse from Solomon's Song of Songs, "I am my beloved's, and my beloved is mine". The speaker is Israel and the beloved is God. Thus, during Elul there is a tangible atmosphere, especially in the synagogue, of the approach of the High Holy Days. This atmosphere is not only the result of inner expectation but is also engendered by several customs. As from the first day (*Rosh Ḥodesh*) of Elul, the ram's horn, *shofar,* is blown at the end of the morning service.

Various reasons are given for this custom. One is that on *Moses on Mt.* *Rosh Ḥodesh* Elul Moses went up to Mount Sinai for the second *Sinai* time to receive the Ten Commandments, having broken the first

1

tablets when he saw the sin of the Golden Calf. He did not descend again until Yom Kippur and the Israelites who awaited his return blew the *shofar* in the camp to remind themselves not to relapse into idol worship again.

A more practical reason is that the *shofar* was also used in war (as a trumpet), and its stirring notes arouse a feeling of apprehension. That is the keynote of Elul — to arouse people from their apathy, shake their equanimity and set in motion the train of thought leading to a heightened spiritual awareness. Except for

A Yemenite blowing the *shofar* at the Western Wall during Elul.

the Sabbaths, the *shofar* is blown every day until the day preceding Rosh Ha-Shanah. This day marks a break between those soundings of the *shofar* which are only a matter of custom and those which are statutory, for blowing the *shofar* on Rosh Ha-Shanah is a biblical injunction (see page 23).

Psalm 27

During the month of Elul a special psalm is recited together with the blowing of the *shofar*. This is Psalm 27 in which certain sentences are understood as being indirect references to Rosh Ha-Shanah and Yom Kippur. The psalm opens with the words, "The Lord is my light and my salvation, of whom shall I be afraid." The words "my light" are taken to refer to Rosh Ha-Shanah, whereas "my salvation" is a reference to the Day of Atonement. When the psalmist continues, "For He concealeth me in His pavilion *(sukkah)* . . .", he brings to mind the festival of Sukkot. The psalm is therefore recited daily until the last day of Sukkot. Quite aside from these midrashic allusions, the theme of the psalm is God's deliverance of David from his enemies, and David's yearning for God's peace. The cry for help and the reliance of the psalmist on God, his longing for God's redemption, "That I may dwell in the house of the Lord all the days of my life, to behold the graciousness of the Lord . . ." is an expression of the spirit of the Days of Awe.

Seliḥot

A third feature of the month of Elul is the recital of the *seliḥot*. These are special supplicatory prayers, often in verse and replete with many biblical allusions. The thirteen Divine attributes of mercy form the central motif, and are repeated several times: "The Lord, the Lord, God, merciful and gracious, long suffering, and abundant in goodness and truth; keeping mercy unto the thousandth generation, forgiving iniquity and transgression and sin; and acquitting." These attributes were revealed to Moses when he asked God to show him His Divine glory.

The *seliḥot* are recited early in the morning before the morning prayers, often before dawn. In Eastern Europe the beadle would go round the streets while it was still dark knocking on the doors and calling the people to come to *seliḥot*. There is also a custom to recite the *seliḥot* at night and usually the *seliḥot* on the first night are recited late in the evening or after midnight. According to the Sephardi rite the *seliḥot* are recited during the whole month of Elul. The Ashkenazi rite, however, begins *seliḥot* only on the Saturday night prior to Rosh Ha-Shanah unless the festival begins on a Monday or Tuesday (it cannot begin on a Sunday), in which case *seliḥot* are recited as from the week before. *Seliḥot* continue to be recited until Yom Kippur although certain rites such as that of the adherents of Ḥabad do not recite them after Rosh Ha-Shanah.

Front page of *Sefer Seliḥot* by Rabbi Abraham bar Yiẓḥak Averbach, printed in Amsterdam by Joseph Athias, 1677.

4

Greeting Cards

In this century the custom has developed of sending greeting cards to friends and relatives for Rosh Ha-Shanah. This practice, which is presumably influenced by secular custom and by commercial interests, has become an integral element of the preparations for the festival although it was not widely known in oriental Jewish communities.

The cards feature the Rosh Ha-Shanah greeting (see page 18), and in earlier years were usually decorated with traditional motifs or the symbols connected with the festival. Nowadays, however, many cards are in the modern fashion and feature pop art or even cartoon strip characters without any connection at all to the festival, other than the greeting.

Assorted greeting cards for Rosh Ha-Shanah.

In Israel, a few weeks before Rosh Ha-Shanah, stalls are set up in the streets selling a bewildering variety of cards, some of which are decorated with portraits of political or military leaders. There are even cards in which the decoration consists of pictures of tanks and jet planes. The Israel Ministry of Communications has to make special arrangements every year to handle the immense volume of cards sent through the mails.

2. ROSH HA-SHANAH

It Is A Day Of Blowing The Horn Unto You

Historical Development

Surprisingly, the name Rosh Ha-Shanah is not found in the Bible. *In the Bible* This name of the festival is normally translated as New Year although the literal and more correct meaning is Head of the Year. It is by the name of Rosh Ha-Shanah that the first of Tishrei has become rooted in Jewish tradition. In the Pentateuch, the festival is mentioned only twice, once in Leviticus where it is called "a solemn rest . . . a memorial proclaimed with the blast of horns, a holy convocation . . .", and again in Numbers where the festival is once more associated with the blowing of the horn: "And in the seventh month, on the first day of the month, ye shall have a holy convocation, ye shall do no manner of servile work; it is a day of blowing the horn unto you." Apart from the sacrifices which are enumerated in the passage in Numbers, it is the *shofar* which, in both instances, is the major theme of the festival. In other parts of the Bible three incidents, all historical, are associated with Rosh Ha-Shanah. The first of these is the murder of Gedaliah, son of Ahikam. After the destruction of the first Temple in 586 b.c.e., the king of Babylon nominated Gedaliah governor of the country. Ishmael, of the Judean royal

6

The Rosh Ha-Shanah service showing the *ḥazzan*, the *shofar* blower, and the "caller", Germany, 1530 (left). *Shofar* from Germany, 18th century (right).

family, came to Gedaliah at Miẓpah and murdered him as they were partaking of a meal together. Actually the Bible only states, "in the seventh month", but, according to tradition this happened on Rosh Ha-Shanah. The murder of Gedaliah led to the final (self) exile of the few Jews remaining in Ereẓ Israel to Egypt. Another event associated with Rosh Ha-Shanah is the rebuilding of the altar in Jerusalem, after the return from the Babylonian exile. Here also there is no specific mention of Rosh Ha-Shanah, although tradition ascribes the event to that festival. The Bible simply states, "And when the seventh month was

7

come . . .". The third event is the great convocation, "upon the first day of the seventh month", held in the time of Ezra and Nehemiah. At this meeting Ezra read to the people from the Bible, "From early morning until midday", and, when the people began to weep, Nehemiah stressed to them the sanctity of the day. Moreover, he encouraged them: "Go your way, eat the fat and drink the sweet; and send portions unto him for whom nothing is prepared; for this day is holy unto the Lord, neither be ye grieved, for the joy of the Lord is your strength." A further indirect reference to Rosh Ha-Shanah is understood by the rabbis in Psalm 81:4–5: "Blow the horn at the new moon, in the time appointed for our feast day. For it is a statute for Israel, an ordinance of the God of Jacob." Here too the biblical theme of blowing the horn is expressed as well as the fact that it is a "feast day".

Blowing the *shofar*, during the synagogue service on Rosh Ha-Shanah. Drawing by Bernard Picart, 1724.

8

In the light of its importance in the Jewish year, the paucity of information about Rosh Ha-Shanah in the Bible seems surprising; it must, however, be remembered that some of the basic tenets of Jewish life and some of the most elementary customs which have been the key to Jewish survival, are hardly mentioned in the written law but have been transmitted orally. This is the case of ritual slaughter *(sheḥitah)*, and many of the laws of the Sabbath, as well as of Rosh Ha-Shanah. In the biblical text itself the only theme that emerges is the *shofar*, proclaiming a "memorial". The oral tradition of the sages, however, associated the sounding of the *shofar* with a triple line of thought which gives the festival three different major meanings: as the anniversary of the world's creation, as the day of judgement, and as a day of renewing the bond between God and Israel.

Although it is generally accepted that Rosh Ha-Shanah is the day of Creation, the rabbis of the Talmud were not fully agreed on this. Two of the greatest sages of their day, Rabbi Joshua and Rabbi Eliezer (1st century c.e.), differed on the subject: According to Rabbi Joshua the world was created in the spring, on the first of Nisan; whereas Rabbi Eliezer maintained that it was created on the first of Tishrei. Even according to the latter view, however, Rosh Ha-Shanah does not represent the first day of Creation but the sixth day when Adam was created.

Rosh Ha-Shanah is also the day of judgement. Every human being is judged individually and his actions are weighed. Similarly, every group — family, community, and nation — is judged, and its fate for the coming year decided. Jewish thought attaches great importance to the individual, who is held responsible not only for his own actions but also for the fate of the community. His good deeds are a credit to the community and his failings or transgressions a debit. Thus, the fate of the whole world rests upon the individual's deeds, for, if the good and evil in the world

9

A page from the *Dresden Maḥzor*, South Germany, c. 1300, depicting the zodiac signs for the months of Elul and Tishrei. The latter shows a good soul being weighed helped by an angel while Evil vainly attempts to pull down its side of the scales.

are evenly balanced, one deed, by a single individual, can be decisive.

These two themes of Rosh Ha-Shanah are universal. The third theme is national, and stresses the direct association of God with Israel, and Israel with God. Israel remembers its obligations as a "unique" nation, and God remembers the promises He made to the Patriarchs and the sacrifice that Abraham was prepared to make when he bound his son, Isaac, on the altar. The bond is thus reciprocal, for while Israel is indebted to God for its very existence, God is also committed to the preservation of His people.

10

"The Sacrifice of Isaac" by Rembrandt, 1655.

In the Bible, Rosh Ha-Shanah is a one day festival, "In the seventh month, on the first day of the month." In practice, however, Rosh Ha-Shanah is celebrated for two days. This is because of the method originally used for determining the beginning of a new month.

The Jewish month follows the lunar cycle (the time it takes the moon to circle the earth) which is approximately 29½ days. The month therefore has either 29 or 30 days, but never more than 30. Tradition required that the new month be determined not by mathematical calculation, but by the evidence of eye witnesses who had seen the "new moon" (the first re-appearance of the moon in the sky as it once again began to wax). Accordingly, people would look out for the new moon on the night of the 29th–30th. The following day, the 30th, the Sanhedrin (the High Court) would receive the witnesses, and, even if they arrived late in the afternoon would declare that day to be *Rosh Ḥodesh,* the first of the new month. This declaration, which was at the same time a sanctification, for *Rosh Ḥodesh* was a semi-festival, would be retroactive and include the whole day. In this case the previous month would have had only 29 days and be termed an "incomplete" month. If no witnesses arrived on the 30th, or if their evidence proved unacceptable, then the month would be a "full" month of 30 days and the following day, the 31st, would automatically become *Rosh Ḥodesh,* the first of the next month.

The exact date of *Rosh Ḥodesh* is important because the dates of the festivals are dependent on it. Immediately after declaring *Rosh Ḥodesh,* the Sanhedrin would set about proclaiming the month to the Jewish communities. This was originally done by a chain of bonfires lit on a series of high mountains. In this way the information also reached the Diaspora. The system broke down owing to the interference of the Samaritans, who used to light the bonfires in order to mislead the Jewish

12

communities. The Sanhedrin then had to rely on messengers, sent from Jerusalem, but these could not reach the Diaspora (Babylon) in time for the festivals of Pesaḥ and Sukkot. As the Jews in the Diaspora remained uncertain as to whether the previous month had been "full" or "incomplete" they were forced to celebrate two days to cover both possibilities. This is the origin of the "second day of *yom tov*" celebrated in the Diaspora.

Rosh Ha-Shanah posed a similar problem which concerned even the Ereẓ Israel communities. It was impossible to know in advance whether witnesses would be forthcoming on the 30th of Elul or not. Owing to this possibility and the subsequent retroactive sanctification, the whole of the 30th day was observed as Rosh Ha-Shanah. If no witnesses appeared, the next day was observed as Rosh Ha-Shanah as well. In this way Rosh Ha-Shanah was frequently observed for two days. Outside Jerusalem people could not know whether Rosh Ha-Shanah had been proclaimed and would observe both days, a custom which became generally accepted.

It seems that even in Temple times the sages knew by calculation the exact time and position of the new moon, but this scientific knowledge was used only for the purpose of verifying the witnesses' evidence. In 359 c.e., the political situation forced the abandonment of the traditional method which was replaced by a mathematically calculated calendar. In Ereẓ Israel the custom of observing Rosh Ha-Shanah for only one day was reintroduced, and this lasted until about the 12th century. At this time, immigrants from the Jewish center of Provence, southern France, settled in Ereẓ Israel and enforced the general custom of two days. Since then Rosh Ha-Shanah has been observed for two days even in Ereẓ Israel, although the other festivals are celebrated for only one. In modern times, the Reform rite the world

13

over has reverted to observing only one day of Rosh Ha-Shanah.

Another rule that gradually developed (after 300 c.e.) was that the first day of Rosh Ha-Shanah must not fall on a Sunday, Wednesday or Friday. This was done in order to avoid the inconvenience of Yom Kippur falling on a day which immediately preceded or followed the Sabbath; or Hoshanah Rabbah (the twenty-first of the month) falling on a Sabbath which would entail the cancellation of the ancient *hoshanah* ceremony in

The title page of Tractate *Rosh Ha-Shanah*, printed in Amsterdam, 1700-1704. It depicts the sighting of the new moon and the lighting of bonfires.

which willow branches were carried in procession and beaten on the ground. During the period when *Rosh Ḥodesh* was still fixed by eye-witnesses, stratagems were sometimes employed in order to prevent the above possibilities; the hearing of the evidence would be prolonged so as not to finish before sunset, in which case the next day would be proclaimed as Rosh Ha-Shanah, or shortened so that the thirtieth could be proclaimed as Rosh Ha-Shanah.

14

Rosh Ha-Shanah was not only the "Head of the Year" from
the ethical-theological point of view but also the beginning of the
new year for certain halakhic purposes. The years were counted
as from Rosh Ha-Shanah with regard to all written contractual
undertakings which had to show a date, such as bills of debt or
divorce documents. The seventh and fiftieth years in the cycle of
seven and fifty years (*shemittah* and *yovel* respectively) — it is
doubtful whether the latter was ever really observed — began
with Rosh Ha-Shanah and not with Nisan. Rosh Ha-Shanah also

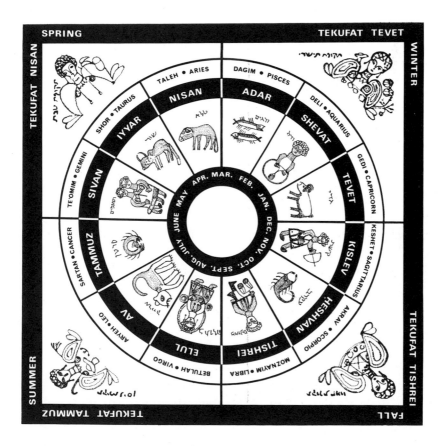

The months of the year on the zodiacal wheel, from the mosaic floor of
the Bet Alpha synagogue, 6th century.

marks the beginning of the year with regard to the law of *orlah,* the fruit of a tree which is forbidden for the first three years of the tree's growth. If the tree was planted early enough to have taken root by Rosh Ha-Shanah, the festival marked the beginning of the second year of its life. For the tithe of corn (cereals) and vegetables, and according to one opinion also of animals, Rosh Ha-Shanah represents a new year, and tithes cannot be set aside from last year's crop for the new year's crop, or vice versa.

The first of Tishrei is not the only New Year in the Jewish year. The sages counted three other such days, each of which was a New Year's day for a particular purpose. The first of Nisan marked a new year in the reign of a Jewish king; a king who ascended the throne in the previous month of Adar would begin the second year of his reign after ruling less than a month. The first of Elul was the new year for animal tithes; sheep and cattle were tithed annually and animals born in one year could not be tithed together with those born in another year. The first, or the fifteenth of Shevat according to the opinion of the disciples of Hillel, was the new year for the tithes of fruit. Of the four new year days mentioned in the Mishnah, the first of Tishrei is obviously the most important. Of the others, only the fifteenth of Shevat has retained any traces of a festival. Known as Tu bi-Shevat (*Tu* = 15), it is celebrated in Israel by tree planting ceremonies and round the world, by the partaking of different types of fruit particularly the seven species for which Erez Israel is famed: wheat, barley, olives, dates, grapes, figs and pomegranates.

Laws and Customs
Although Rosh Ha-Shanah and Yom Kippur are the most serious and inspiring days in the Jewish year they do not lose their atmosphere of festivity. Even Yom Kippur, the day of fast and

affliction, remains a Sabbath. So too, Rosh Ha-Shanah, despite the fact that it is the day of judgement, is nevertheless regarded as a festival. This is given expression by several customs whose inspiration is the confidence that God's judgement is tempered by His mercy.

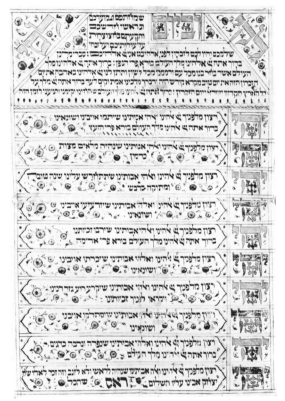

Rosh Ha-Shanah tablet from Persia, 18th century, listing symbolic benedictions recited during the evening meal.

On *erev* Rosh Ha-Shanah, the day preceding the festival, it is usual to bathe, cut one's hair, and wear Sabbath clothes in the evening. On the other hand many people observe a half day fast on *erev* Rosh Ha-Shanah and after the morning prayers, when the *seliḥot* are exceptionally long, it is usual to assemble in

Erev Rosh Ha-Shanah

groups of three which sit down to form *adhoc* courts. The others then ask the "court" to nullify any vows made consciously or unintentionally during the past year, and declare that all future vows and good intentions concerning oneself shall be void. False or unfulfilled oaths and vows have always been considered major sins. The *halakhah* recognizes numerous categories of oaths and vows, mostly distinguished one from the other by the terminology used. In most periods of Jewish history it was both customary and of frequent occurence to make vows of good intention or pious resolution as well as for thanksgiving or when beseeching divine help; human weakness often left these unfulfilled. It was also fairly easy for a person to express himself quite unintentionally in vow terminology. A person might express a pious wish, or even simply make a mental resolve to observe a certain meritorious custom, which if observed three times in succession would automatically assume the validity of a vow. For this reason it is considered so important to receive annulment of both intentional and unintentional vows before the day of judgement so as not to come before God with outstanding vows. This ceremony is repeated by the congregation as a whole in the opening *Kol Nidrei* service on Yom Kippur eve (see page 70).

At the synagogue service on Rosh Ha-Shanah many congregants wear a white garment over their Sabbath clothes or some white articles of clothing, whether a *kippah* (skullcap) or a white tie. White is the symbol of purity and a white overgarment is also reminiscent of a shroud and, by evoking death, induces the attitude of humble supplication befitting the occasion.

The Evening of Rosh Ha-Shanah

Following the evening service, as people leave the synagogue, a special form of greeting is used: "May you be inscribed (in the Book of Life) for a good year."

The festive meal in the evening opens with the *Kiddush* which is followed by a series of acts, symbolic that the coming year may be one of happiness and success both for the individual, and for the Jewish people as a whole. The bread, normally dipped in salt, is dipped in honey to betoken a "sweet" year. For the same reason an apple is also dipped in honey and the wish, "May it by Thy will that this year will be a happy and sweet year" is recited. More symbolic acts follow, varying according to the rites of the different communities. The seeds of a pomegranate are eaten with the accompanying prayer that God may multiply the credit of our good deeds. Headmeat, preferably of a ram in memory of the Binding of Isaac, or even fish heads, are eaten with the hope that "we may be the head and not the tail." It is also the custom not to eat anything bitter or even vinegary on Rosh Ha-Shanah eve. Nor are nuts eaten, because the word "nut" is numerically equal to "sin". (In Hebrew each letter has also a numerical value; *egoz* (nut) = 17, *het* (sin) = 18. In numerical equations, one, standing for the word itself, is often added or subtracted). A more logical reason for not eating nuts is that they irritate the throat and make speech, needed for prayer on the morrow, more difficult.

The historical development of Rosh Ha-Shanah which led to the celebration of two days has halakhic consequences for the customs on the second night of Rosh Ha-Shanah.

The She-heheyanu Benediction

Every festival is sanctified with the *she-heheyanu* benediction: "Blessed art Thou, O Lord our God, King of the Universe, who has kept us in life, and has preserved us and enabled us to reach this season."

This benediction is recited by the woman when lighting the candles and by the man during the *Kiddush.* (On Yom Kippur which is a fast day when no *Kiddush* is made the benediction is recited by the congregation in unison in the synagogue prior to the evening service proper.) The two days of Rosh Ha-Shanah are considered halakhically as one long day; for originally if the witnesses, testifying to having seen the moon, came in the afternoon of the first day, the second day was nevertheless observed. Yet in reality, only one of the two days can really be New Year's day. The question therefore arises whether the *she-heheyanu* benediction should be recited for the second day or not. The problem is resolved by a "halakhicism". A new garment is worn, or a fruit which has as yet not been eaten (tasted) is placed on the table. Either of these would normally require a *she-heheyanu* benediction in their own right. In this instance the *she-heheyanu* is recited when lighting the candles and during the *Kiddush* but with the garment or fruit in mind as well. The fruit is then eaten immediately after the partaking of the bread. If no new garment or fruit is available the *she-heheyanu* benediction is nevertheless recited. Similarly, the *she-heheyanu* is recited prior to the *shofar* blowing on the second day, although in this case there is an opinion which maintains that the *she-heheyanu* for the *shofar* is said on the second day only if the first day of Rosh Ha-Shanah falls on a Sabbath when the *shofar* is not sounded. There is also a difference of opinion as to whether the special greeting is used on the second night, but the accepted custom is to use the same greeting on both nights.

A widely practiced custom on Rosh Ha-Shanah is the *Tashlikh* ceremony. This is performed by reciting several supplicatory prayers at a source of water, such as a well, spring, river or at the sea-shore. Afterwards, the pockets are symbolically emptied as if a person is shaking off his sins and casting them into the water. As a source for this ceremony the verses in Micah are often quoted: "He will again have compassion upon us; He will subdue our iniquities; and Thou wilt cast all their sins into the depth of the sea."

The Tashlikh Ceremony

There are other, more homiletic, explanations for going to a body of water. The water reminds us of Abraham's self-sacrifice

20

The *Tashlikh* ceremony performed at a well (right). The *Tashlikh* ceremony on the edge of the Mediterranean Sea, Tel Aviv (below).

in the story of the Binding of Isaac. According to the Midrash, Satan attempted to prevent Abraham from carrying out God's command and turned himself into a raging river. Abraham began to ford the river, and when the water came up to his neck, he called on God for help. The waters immediately subsided. Another reason is that Jewish kings were always crowned near a spring, itself a symbol of continuity; on Rosh Ha-Shanah, Israel crowns

Reciting the *Tashlikh* prayer, drawing by Marc Chagall.

the Eternal King. In Europe, it was the custom to go to a river or stream in which there were fish which also have a symbolic significance. They have no eyelids and God is beseeched to watch constantly over His people; man cannot escape God's judgement just as fish caught in the fisherman's net cannot escape; the "evil eye" has no power over the fish in the water; and fish are the accepted symbol of fertility.

It is unknown when the *Tashlikh* custom first developed. It is mentioned at the beginning of the 15th century by Jacob Mollin, the famous author whose work cites many ancient Jewish customs of Germany. The *Tashlikh* ceremony is, however, widespread and not confined to Ashkenazi communities. It was nevertheless opposed by certain rabbinical authorities such as Elijah, the Gaon of Vilna, as smacking of superstition.

Tashlikh is performed on the first day of Rosh Ha-Shanah in the afternoon after the *Minḥah* service. When the first day falls on a Sabbath the ceremony is deferred to the second day, probably because the people could not carry their prayerbooks to the stream on the Sabbath. In Jerusalem, the ceremony used to be carried out next to the numerous water cisterns in the city; since the Six-Day War, the traditional *Tashlikh* site next to the Gihon spring in the Shiloah Valley, where Solomon was crowned, has again become extremely popular.

A "Shul-klapper" (wooden mallet) shaped like a *shofar*, used for knocking on doors to awaken the congregants for *seliḥot*. Note the carved eagle at one end in accordance with the admonition, "be as light as an eagle...to do the will of thy Father." (*Avot* 5:23)

The Shofar

In the Bible, Rosh Ha-Shanah is described as a "day of sounding the horn", and the central ceremony of the festival is sounding

Sounding the Shofar

the *shofar.* Traditionally, a ram's horn is used as a reminder of the ram which Abraham sacrificed in place of Isaac. The *halakhah,* however, permits any horn from a kosher animal except that of an ox or cow. The latter are termed *keren* in Hebrew and are therefore excluded from the true *shofar* category. A midrashic explanation for the inacceptability of the horn of oxen is that the ox recalls Israel's greatest sin, the Golden Calf, and a prosecutor cannot at the same time serve as defending counsel.

The *shofar* should be curved, a symbol that man must bend his will before God. It is usually softened and shaped in hot

24

Silver gilt breastplate with jewelled crown. The centerpiece, containing the inscription *Yom Kippur* could be opened, and on each holiday the appropriate engraved plaque bearing the holiday's name was inserted. Munich, Germany, 1826 (left).

17th century silver Torah breastplate, partly gilt and inlaid with semi-precious stones. The center inscription reads *Rosh Ha-Shanah*; this breastplate was used as a Torah ornament solely on that Holy Day. Hamburg, Germany (right).

Rosh Ha-Shanah plate, Delft, Holland, c. 1700. The plate was used for the apple dipped in honey consumed on that festival to betoken a sweet year.

Delft plate, 18th century Holland. Faience, with the words *Hasimah Tovah*, "a favorable inscription". This plate was used to serve the *hallah* and honey during the festive meal preceding the Atonement fast. Of interest is the spelling error in the word *Hasimah*.

water. There must be no impairment in the sound the *shofar* produces; a split or hole in the *shofar* is liable to render it unfit. It is not always easy to blow the *shofar,* and some are extremely difficult. Often the *ba'al teki'ah* or *ba'al toke'ah,* as the sounder of the horn is called, keeps a reserve *shofar* at hand. It is a feat of strength and endurance to blow the whole series of notes successfully, and much practice is usually needed. Nevertheless, the *ba'al teki'ah* occasionally finds himself unable to continue, and is replaced by another. Since the sounding of the *shofar* is understood as calling forth God's mercy on His creatures who stand before Him in prayer, great stress is placed on the *ba'al teki'ah's* piety as well as on his ability. In order to avoid confusion as to which sound to blow, the *ba'al teki'ah* is accompanied by the *makri* (the "caller"), usually the rabbi of the community, who quietly calls out the note to be sounded. Both the blower and the caller have to be well versed in the complicated rules of the notes, the length and types of sound, and the way they must be blown. The listeners must hear the actual sound of the *shofar* and not its echo. Halakhically, it is inadmissable to hear the *shofar* with the aid of a loudspeaker or over the radio. The normal place for blowing the *shofar* in the synagogue is the central *bimah,* from which the Torah is also read.

Before blowing the *shofar* the congregation recites Psalm 47 seven times. The psalm exalts God as King of all the earth, a befitting theme for blowing the *shofar.* It also includes the verse: "God is gone up amidst shouting, The Lord amidst the sound of the *shofar.*" This verse is given as the reason for holding the *shofar* with the wide end pointing upwards. Psalm 47 is followed by the verse: "Out of the straits I called upon the Lord, He answered me with great enlargement."

Another six verses are then recited, the first letters of each verse form an acrostic, reading: *kera satan,* "Tear up Satan".

A page from an Italian *mahzor* listing the first group of *shofar* blowings (left). The title page of the first prayer book for the High Holy Days published in the American Colonies, New York, 1761 (opposite).

Satan personifies the power of evil in the world; the *shofar*, the establishment of God's kingdom on earth.

After the preliminary Bible verses, the Reader recites the benedictions for blowing the *shofar*. The first benediction has halakhic significance for it is not "Who hath commanded us to blow the *shofar*" but "to hear the sound of the *shofar*". Although a certain rabbinic opinion maintained that the essence of the commandment was to blow the *shofar*, the accepted opinion is that the biblical injunction is to hear the *shofar*. As a

26

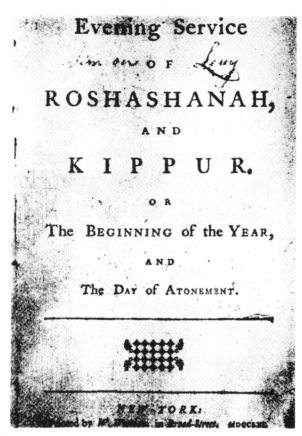

Evening Service OF ROSHASHANAH, AND KIPPUR. OR The BEGINNING of the YEAR, AND The DAY of ATONEMENT.

NEW YORK:

result of this ruling, a deaf person is absolved from observing the commandment despite the fact that he could blow the *shofar* himself. There is also a moral implication to this ruling: it is insufficient to sound the call to repentance, one must heed the call.

The sounding of the *shofar* falls into two groups. The first group precedes the *Musaf* prayer and is called the "sitting sounds", because originally it was permitted to remain seated when hearing these. The second group is blown during the *Musaf*

27

service and is connected with the specific Rosh Ha-Shanah prayers (see page 37). According to the Ashkenazi rite the second group is blown only during and following the reader's repetition of the *Musaf Amidah*, (*Amidah* is the prayer of silent benedictions). Sephardi and ḥasidic rite requires the *shofar* to be blown during the silent *Amidah* of *Musaf* as well.

There is some doubt as to the exact type of sound required by the biblical injunction so that different forms are used to cover the various possibilities. The "wailing" note is always preceded and followed by a long clear blast (*teki'ah*). The "wailing" or "sobbing" note is one of three alternatives: three short blasts of the horn (*shevarim*), or a series of extremely short blasts (*teru'ah*), or a combination of the two, three short blasts followed by a series of staccato notes (*shevarim-teru'ah*). As each is repeated three times, this makes a total of 30 blasts (thrice *teki'ah shevarim-teru'ah teki'ah*, thrice *teki'ah shevarim teki'ah*, and thrice *teki'ah teru'ah teki'ah*). In addition to the 30 blasts blown before the *Musaf* service, another 60 blasts are blown during *Musaf.* The last *teki'ah* blast is drawn out and is called *teki'ah gedolah*, the "great *teki'ah*". It evokes the long sounding of the horn after God's appearance on Sinai, which signified that the Divine Presence had gone up from the mountain: "When the ram's horn soundeth long, they shall come up to the mount". On Rosh Ha-Shanah, too, the long *teki'ah* marks the conclusion of the *shofar* sounds as commanded in the Bible. In order to round off the number of blasts to 100, a further 10 notes are blown at the conclusion of the service.

Rav Hai Gaon (died 1035) explained the fact that although the *shofar* was blown every year, doubt arose as to the correct note to be sounded by the *shofar*. He suggested that for years people had sounded the "wailing" note, some shorter and some longer until the time of Rabbi Abbahu (3rd/4th century), who ordained that all Israel should conform to a uniform system of notes in order that the ignorant should not think that there were differences in the observance of the law.

Women

The biblical injunction of blowing the *shofar* is a commandment dependent on time (i.e., Rosh Ha-Shanah), and there is a ruling that all commandments which are limited by a time factor are not applicable to women. In the case of the *shofar*, however, as with certain other commandments, women have nevertheless accepted the injunction. They are thus obliged to hear the *shofar*; if they are unable to attend the synagogue it is customary to blow it for them at home.

The Time of Blowing the Shofar

The *shofar* can be blown the entire day. Normally the rabbis recommend an early observance of a commandment. In the case of the *shofar*, however, historical events caused the normal time to be fixed later in the day, before and during the *Musaf* service. Rabbi Johanan (3rd century c.e.) related that once when the Jews blew the *shofar*, the enemy. (presumably the Romans) thought that the trumpetings heralded a revolt, and immediately fell upon the Jews. The sages thereupon ordained that the *shofar* be blown only later in the day; the Romans would see that the Jews were praying in the synagogue and reading the Law, and would consequently realize that the *shofar* was a part of the religious service, and not a call to arms.

The Temple and Sabbath

In the Temple the *shofar* was accompanied by the blasts of two silver trumpets, positioned one on either side of the *shofar*. The sound of the *shofar* continued after the trumpets had stopped as the biblical injunction stressed the sound of the *shofar*. Less than a century after the destruction of the Temple, opinion was divided as to what type of horn was used in the Temple for the *shofar*. One view was that it was fashioned from the horn of the ibex, while another view held it to have been a ram's horn. Even during Temple times, the *shofar* was blown (without the

דקדשא בריך הוא לעילא מכל ברכתא ושירתא תושׁבחתא
תושבחתא ונחמתא דאמירן בעלמא ואמרו
אמן

ברכו את יי המבורך

ברוך יי המבורך לעולם ועד

ברוך אתה יי אלהינו מלך

העולם יוצר אור ובורא חשך עושה
שלום ובורא את הכל אור עולם באוצר
חיים אורות מאופל אמר ויהי

Page from the *Leipzig Mahzor* depicting the *hazzan* and two of the congregants standing behind or beside him. They wear Jews' hats. South Germany, c. 1320.

accompaniment of the trumpets) in all communal centers as well. On the Sabbath, however, the *shofar* was blown only in the Temple (and, according to Maimonides, throughout Jerusalem). Following the destruction of the Temple, Rabbi Johanan ben Zakkai ordained that the *shofar* should be blown on the Sabbath wherever the Sanhedrin was sitting. With the discontinuation of the Sanhedrin, the Sabbath *shofar* blowing was also discontinued. An application of Rabbi Johanan ben Zakkai's ruling was, however, carried out by Rabbi Isaac Alfasi (1012–1103) who blew the *shofar* when Rosh Ha-Shanah coincided with the Sabbath. At the beginning of this century (1905–1906), Rabbi Akiva Joseph Schlesinger attempted, unsuccessfully, with the use of various halakhic arguments, to renew the custom and was said to have blown the *shofar* on Sabbath in the privacy of his own home. His efforts caused a communal uproar in Jerusalem.

The sages point to a biblical source for the difference between Sabbath and weekdays. In Numbers, the festival is des-

30

A double page from a written *maḥzor* with the *Melekh Elyon piyyut*.

cribed as "a day of blowing the horn". In Leviticus, however, it is called "a memorial of blowing [the horn]". On weekdays, so the sages explained, Rosh Ha-Shanah was a "day of blowing" but on the Sabbath it was only "a memorial of blowing". Only in the Temple where "ye shall bring an offering" was the blowing of the *shofar* permitted on the Sabbath.

Due to the biblical emphasis, the *shofar* has become the *Significance and* symbol of Rosh Ha-Shanah, just as *mazzah* symbolizes Pesaḥ and *Symbolism* the *lulav* and *etrog* symbolize Sukkot. The symbol became so popular in ancient times, that, together with the *lulav* and *etrog* and the *menorah* (the seven-branched candelabrum of the Temple), it became a leading motif in Jewish art. The significance of blowing the *shofar,* passed over in silence in the Bible, has intrigued Jewish thinkers throughout the ages. The most explicit treatment of the question was given by Sa'adiah Gaon (892–942) who gave ten reasons for sounding the *shofar* on Rosh Ha-Shanah.

1. Rosh Ha-Shanah as the day of Creation is the anniversary of God's rule. It is a coronation day, and Israel, as God's people, proclaim His kingship.

2. Rosh Ha-Shanah introduces the Ten Days of Penitence and the *shofar* calls for repentance.

3. The *shofar* evokes the revelation at Sinai, when the Torah was given to Israel amidst the blowing of the horn.

4. The sound of the *shofar* is compared to the inspiring message of the prophet: "When I bring the sword upon a land, if the people of the land take a man from among them, and set him for their watchman; if when he seeth the sword come upon the land, he bloweth the horn and warneth the people; then whosoever heareth the sound of the horn and taketh not warning . . . his blood shall be upon him; whereas if he had taken warning, he would have delivered his soul. But if the watchman seeth the sword come and bloweth not the horn and the people be not warned . . . his blood will I require at the watchman's hand. So thou, son of man, I have set thee a watchmen unto the house of Israel, therefore, when thou shalt hear the word at My mouth warn them from Me . . .".

5. The *shofar* is the sound of battle and the clash of arms. The memory of the capture of Jerusalem and the destruction of the Temple evoke prayers for the speedy return of our national glory.

6. The *shofar* is symbolic of the ram Abraham sacrificed instead of Isaac. Abraham was prepared to offer up his beloved child at God's command and Isaac, too, when it became clear that he himself was the chosen sacrifice, did not hesitate or doubt God's righteousness. The trials of the Patriarchs remain an

inspiration to the Jewish people and stand to Israel's credit when they are judged every year.

7. The sound of the horn arouses fear: "Shall the horn be blown in a city and the people not tremble . . .?"

8. The *shofar* evokes the ultimate Day of Judgement: "The great day of the Lord is near, it is near and hasteth greatly . . . a day of the horn and alarm . . ."

9. The final Ingathering of the Exiles is also associated with the blowing of the horn: "And it shall come to pass on that day, that a great horn shall be blown; and they shall come that were lost in the land of Assyria, and they that were dispersed in the land of Egypt; and they shall worship the Lord in the holy mountain at Jerusalem."

10. The *shofar* is connected with the Resurrection. It is in this sense that the verse in Isaiah was interpreted: "All ye inhabitants of the world, and ye dwellers in the earth, when an ensign is lifted up on the mountains, see ye; and when the horn is blown, hear ye."

Despite Sa'adiah's seemingly complete treatment of the subject, the rabbis continued to discuss the meaning of the *shofar*. Moses Maimonides, one of the greatest Jewish minds of the Middle Ages, gives a very simple, straightforward explanation. The *shofar* is a call: "Awake, you sleepers, from your sleep and you slumberers awake from your slumber. Reflect on your deeds and repent, and remember your Creator. Look to your souls and mend your ways and actions, those who forget the truth because of the empty vanities of life, who all their years go astray following vanity and folly which neither profit nor save. An let each one of you abandon his evil way and thoughts which are not good."

A beautiful parable was given by the famous ḥasidic sage, Levi Isaac of Berdichev. "A king was once lost in a forest and no one was able to show him the way out. Then the king saw a wise old man who recognized him as the king and showed him the way. The king was grateful to the wise man and rewarded him, raising him to a high position in the realm. Many years later the wise man provoked the king's displeasure, and when called to trial appeared wearing the same clothes he had worn on his first meeting with the king. Seeing him again in that ragged attire, the king remembered his original meeting with the old man, and remembering, forgave him." Similarly, said Rabbi Levi Isaac, the sounding of the *shofar* reminds God of Israel's good beginning, of its original free committment at Sinai to accept God's kingship and His Torah.

Liturgy

As is understandable on the Day of Judgement, supplication occupies a major place on Rosh Ha-Shanah and in most communities more than half the day is spent in prayer at the synagogue. It is related in the Talmud in the name of Rabbi Johanan (3rd century c.e.) that three books are open before God on Rosh Ha-Shanah. One is the Book of Life in which the names of the just are immediately entered, and confirmed; one is the Book of Death in which the wicked are entered; and the third is the book for those who are neither wholly just nor wholly wicked, in whose case the verdict is delayed until the Day of Atonement. This picturesque description has been the subject of many later interpretations, but, notwithstanding all the ethical and philosophical difficulties entailed, it successfully stresses the idea of judgement being passed on each individual on this day. In a lighter vein, but expressing the inner meaning of the day is the question: How can God write on the festival, for writing is considered a desecration? The answer given is that when life is in danger, everything is permitted. This concept of Rosh Ha-Shanah

The Purpose of Prayer

34

עוֹלָב
קָרָאוּ
אַחֲרָיו
תֵּלְכוּ
לְמוֹרָא
דְּרָשׁוּ
יֵשׁ כְּהֶם
בְּהִמָּצֵא
בְּאֱלֹהִים
יָמִים
לְעֵרוּב

בִּתְשׁוּבָה בָּא לְקָרוֹב · קְרָאוּהוּ בִּהְיוֹתוֹ קָרוֹב : גָּדוֹל וְאֵין נֶעֱרָכוֹ גָּזַר לִי
לִינִיר לְהַאֲרִיכוֹ · וְעֻזּוֹ בְרֶשַׁע דִּרְכּוֹ "
אֵלֵינוּ בְּיַחְטְבוֹתֵיהוּ לְעִי־

Repenting figure from Rothschild Ms., written c. 1470.

explains why, in contrast to the other festivals, the *Hallel* prayer is not recited, for, in the words of Rabbi Abbahu, how can Israel sing hymns of praise when the King is seated on His throne in judgement and human lives hang in the balance!

The general order of service on Rosh Ha-Shanah, with the exception of the *shofar* which follows the Torah reading, is

35

similar to that on Sabbath and other festivals. The morning service is followed by readings from the Torah and Prophets and this is followed by the *Musaf* service. Whereas *Shaḥarit,* the morning service, represents the morning sacrifice in the Temple, which it replaces, *Musaf* represents the additional sacrifices of the day. Torah readings, too, originate from an early period and the principle was probably instituted by Ezra (5th century b.c.e.). Public reading from the Torah was certainly an accepted custom in the Second Temple period.

The outstanding difference between the liturgy of Rosh Ha-Shanah and that of the other festivals is in the *Amidah,* (silent prayer) especially in the *Musaf Amidah* which is the longest of the whole year. Not only does the text differ, but even the manner in which the prayer is recited. Whereas all the year round the *Amidah* must be recited silently so as not to disturb one's neighbors' concentration, on Rosh Ha-Shanah (and on Yom Kippur) it is permitted to say it in a slightly louder voice. It was reasoned that on the High Holy Days everyone uses a prayer book and is less likely to be confused by other voices. It is also customary on the High Holy Days for a person to stand with his head bowed during the *Amidah* as a sign of contrition and humility, except when pronouncing God's name.

The *amidot* are the central points of the service. The third benediction which normally concludes with "Blessed art Thou, O Lord, holy God" is, from Rosh Ha-Shanah until after the Day of Atonement, changed to "Blessed art Thou, O Lord, holy King".

On the High Holy Days, this third benediction of the *Amidah* is expanded and includes a prayer for the realization of God's kingdom on earth. All creatures are to recognize God's rule and a special place is allotted to God's people, to Jerusalem and to the Messiah, descendant of David; evil will be swallowed up and God's reign will be supreme: "Reign over the whole universe in

Thy glory and in Thy splendor be exalted over all the earth . . . that every form may know that Thou has formed it, and every creature understand that Thou has created it."

Here too, God's universal role is stressed side by side with the specific role of God as the creator of a sanctified Israel: "Blessed art Thou, O Lord, King over all the earth Who sanctifiest Israel and the Day of Memorial."

Prior to the *Musaf* service, the *ḥazzan* (cantor) recites an *The Musaf* exceptionally moving personal prayer, partially aloud and *Prayer* partially in silence. It voices his trepidation at leading the congregation in prayer and pleads that his personal failings should not hinder the prayers' acceptance. He concludes his prayer with the benediction "Blessed art Thou Who heareth prayer."

The *Musaf Amidah* at first follows the same pattern as the morning *Amidah*. This is followed by a recitation of the festival's special sacrifices as in all *Musaf amidot*. The remaining part of the *Musaf Amidah* is taken up by a tripartite division. The three parts are termed *Malkhuyyot,* — the exaltation of God as King; *Zikhronot,* — rememberance; and *Shofarot,* — the *shofar*. This division is also responsible for Rosh Ha-Shanah's other three names *Yom ha-Din,* the Day of Judgement; *Yom ha-Zikaron,* the Day of Rememberance; and *Yom Teru'ah,* the Day of Blowing the Horn. This division coincides with the festival's three major themes (see page 9). Each section starts with a short prayer which states the central idea of that section. This is followed by a quotation of ten verses; three from the Pentateuch, three from the Hagiographa, three from the Prophets and a concluding verse again from the Pentateuch. After the verses, a short summation comes ending in a benediction which exemplifies the section. In the reader's repetition, the *shofar* is blown at the conclusion of each section. According to Sephardi and ḥasidic rites, it is also blown at the conclusion of each section in the silent *Amidah*.

בָּרוּךְ אַתָּה יְיָ שׁוֹמֵעַ קוֹל תְּרוּעַת עַמּוֹ יִשְׂו

יִשְׂרָאֵל בְּרַחֲמִים

קִיעָה תְּרוּעָה קִיעָה

הַיּוֹם הֲרַת

עוֹלָם הַיּוֹם יַעֲמִיד

בְּמִשְׁפָּט כָּל יְצוּרֵ ן

עוֹלָמִים אִם כְּבָנִים

אִם כַּעֲבָדִים אִם כְּבָנִ

רַחֲמֵנוּ כְּרַחֵם אָב עַל בָּנִים אִם כַּעֲבָדִים עֵיו

Detail from a 14th century *mahzor* showing the *shofar* blowing. At the side is a terrified Satan.

The tripartite division accompanied by the *shofar* is mentioned in the Mishnah which also requires the recital of ten verses from the Bible, although the verses were not then fixed. The short prayers preceding the quotations are attributed to Rav (3rd century c.e.), the outstanding pupil of Judah ha-Nasi ("Rabbi") who evidently also composed the expanded third benediction (see page 36). The first of these prayers preceding the quotations is *Aleinu le-Shabbe'ah* which stresses God's universal kingship and His choice of Israel. This prayer became so popular that it is recited at the conclusion of every service, all through the year. On Rosh Ha-

38

Shanah and Yom Kippur it is customary in many congregations, to kneel down and bow during the reader's repetition of the words "we bend the knee and prostrate ourselves".

The second section "Rememberances" stresses the concept of Rosh Ha-Shanah as a Day of Judgement when God "remembers" all that has passed: "For there is no forgetfulness before the throne of Thy glory, nor is there aught hidden from Thine eyes." The closing benediction is "Who remembereth the Covenant".

The third section "Shofarot" gives expression to some of the ideas already discussed: the receiving of the Torah at Sinai, the redemption to the sound of the horn, and the Temple service. The final benediction praises God, "Who in mercy heareth the sound of the blowing of his people Israel."

The themes of all three sections are closely related to the sound of the *shofar* as shown by the reasons stated by Sa'adiah Gaon.

In the reader's Repetition of the *Amidah*, both *Shaḥarit* and *Musaf,* the congregation joins in the recital of numerous prayers, composed throughout the Middle Ages, many in verse. These are termed *piyyutim* and the composer, a *paytan.* The *piyyutim* recited differ according to rite and community. In certain communities, the *piyyutim* are reduced to a minimum in order to leave more time for the statutory prayers. Several of the *piyyutim* have become extremely popular. One of the best known is *U-Netanneh Tokef.*

U-Netanneh Tokef is a moving description of judgement day, and concludes with a message of hope that repentance, prayer and charity can change an unfavorable decree.

Legend has it that it was composed by Amnon of Mainz who lived during the 10/11th century. Amnon was an outstanding Jewish figure, respected alike by Jew and non-Jew. He was on especially good terms with the ruler-bishop of Mainz who, at the

U-Netanneh Tokef

39

עובר הרוקע ומברך ברכה אחת לשמיע בקול שופֿי

ומשלש קשׁרֿה מֿשלש תֿשׁרֿהׁ ומשלש תֿרֿי]]]

יפֿתֿיח פֿאסֿרֿי · ומתֿפֿלֿיו הֿיֿנֿיפֿר למֿיסֿח כֿרֿרֿ

שֿהתֿפֿלֿו בֿיׁב רֿאׁשֿׁון · ויֿאֿחֿרֿכֿ אֿיׁכֿ שֿלֿחֿעֿבֿר

בֿרֿיֿכֿ אֿתֿ ⑥ אֿלֿהֿיֿנֿו ואֿלֿי אֿבֿותֿיֿנֿו אֿלֿהֿי אֿבֿ אֿלֿהֿי יֿצֿ ואֿלֿהֿי יֿעֿקֿבֿ עֿד

בֿלֿ עֿוֿזֿר וֿמֿוֿשֿיֿעֿ וֿמֿגֿן ·

לחֿיֿיֿם מֿלֿךֿ חֿפֿץ בֿחֿיֿיֿם · וֿכֿתֿבֿנֿו

בֿסֿפֿר חֿיֿיֿם טֿוֿבֿיֿם לֿמֿעֿנֿךֿ אֿלֿהֿיֿם

חֿיֿיֿם · מֿלֿךֿ עֿוֿזֿר וֿמֿוֿשֿיֿעֿ וֿמֿגֿן · בֿאֿ ⑥ מֿגֿן אֿבֿרֿ

אֿתֿהֿ גֿבֿיֿר לֿעֿוֿלֿם ⑥ ומֿ · עֿד מֿרֿעֿגֿרֿיֿח יֿשֿוֿעֿה ·

כֿמֿוֿכֿה אֿבֿ הֿרֿחֿמֿיֿם · זֿוֿכֿר יֿצֿורֿיֿו לֿחֿיֿיֿם

בֿרֿחֿמֿיֿם · יֿתֿאֿמֿן אֿתֿהֿ לֿהֿחֿיֿת רֿחֿמֿיֿם"

בֿרֿוֿךֿ אֿתֿהֿ ⑥ מֿחֿיֿה הֿמֿתֿיֿם · לֿילֿגֿ ·

קֿדֿיֿשֿתֿהֿיֿם · כֿי הֿיֿא צֿרֿא וֿאֿיֿם · וֿבֿי תֿנֿשֿאֿ

מֿלֿכֿותֿךֿ · רֿיֿכֿוֿ בֿחֿסֿד כֿכֿאֿר · וֿתֿשֿכֿ עֿלֿיֿו בֿאֿמֿתֿ אֿמֿה

כֿי אֿתֿה דֿיֿין וֿמֿוֿכֿיֿח וֿיֿוֿדֿע וֿעֿד וֿכֿותֿב וֿחֿותֿם וֿתֿופֿר

כֿל הֿנֿשֿכֿחֿותֿ וֿתֿפֿתֿח סֿפֿר זֿכֿרֿונֿתֿ · וֿמֿרֿאֿלֿיֿו יֿקֿרֿ

וֿחֿותֿם יֿד כֿל אֿדֿכֿ בֿי · וֿכֿשֿוֿפֿר גֿדֿוֿל יֿתֿקֿע וֿקֿוֿל דֿמֿמֿה

יֿשֿמֿע · וֿמֿיֿלֿאֿכֿיֿם יֿחֿפֿזֿוֿן · חֿיֿל וֿרֿעֿדֿה יֿאֿחֿזֿוֿן וֿיֿאֿמֿרֿו

הֿנֿה יֿוֿם דֿיֿן · לֿפֿקֿוֿד עֿל צֿבֿא מֿרֿוֿם בֿדֿיֿן כֿי לֿא יֿזֿכֿו בֿ

בֿעֿיֿנֿךֿ בֿדֿיֿן · וֿכֿל בֿאֿי עֿוֿלֿם יֿעֿבֿרֿו לֿפֿנֿךֿ כֿבֿנֿי מֿרֿוֿן

כֿבֿקֿרֿתֿ רֿוֿעֿה עֿדֿרֿוֿ · וֿמֿעֿבֿיֿר צֿאֿנֿו תֿחֿתֿ שֿבֿטֿו · כֿן תֿהֿ

A page from the *Great Mahzor of Amsterdam* with *U-Netannah Tokef* in large decorated letters in the center. At the top are instructions for blowing the *shofar* including intonation signs.

Religious accessories usually reserved for High Holy Day use. A silver *tallit* collar (*atarah*) in which each square is inscribed with a word making up the kabbalistic prayer for the donning of the *tallit* and the benediction; Poland, 18th century. Silver belt buckle with hands raised in priestly blessing; Poland, 1825. Cantor's silk skullcap embossed with letters of silver thread; Germany, 18th century.

An illuminated Rosh Ha-Shanah *piyyut* showing the blowing of the *shofar* and an illustration of a ram caught in a thicket, from Volume II of the *Leipzig Maḥzor,* South Germany, c. 1320.

Blowing the *shofar*. A page from the *Rothschild Miscellany*,
written and illuminated in Ferrara, c. 1470. Picture at bottom depicts a man blowing the *shofar* for women listeners.
Inscription under seated listeners reads *Avinu Malkenu*,
"Our Father, Our King", from the High Holy Day liturgy.

insistence of his advisors, continually pressed Amnon to convert to Christianity on the assumption that the whole Jewish community would follow his example. Amnon evaded the issue as best he could but finally promised to give an answer within three days. He immediately regretted his promise since it implied that he was at least ready to consider apostasy. Ashamed of his lapse, Amnon went into seclusion and refused to meet the bishop again. Ultimately, he was brought before him by force, and at once pronounced his own judgement — to have his tongue, which had uttered false words, torn out by the roots. The bishop, greatly angered, answered that his tongue had spoken justly but his hands which refused to accept the new faith, and his feet which refused to come, should be cut off. On Rosh Ha-Shanah, Amnon was carried to the synagogue and his litter set down next to the *hazzan*. When the *hazzan* reached the *Kedushah* prayer, Amnon stopped him and then began *U-Netanneh Tokef*. As he finished, his spirit left his broken body and entered the world to come. Three days later he appeared in a dream to his pupil, Kalonymus ben Meshullam, taught him the prayer, and commanded him to teach it to others so that it might always be recited on the High Holy Days.

The Torah Readings

In Ashkenazi communities a special chant is used for the Torah readings on the High Holy Days which is more solemn than that used during the year. *The Melody*

The passages selected for reading on the two days of Rosh Ha-Shanah are consecutive and actually form a single narrative episode (Genesis, Ch. 21, 22). Whereas the Torah readings on the Sabbath are arranged in sequence so as to complete the Pentateuch in one year, the readings on festivals always have a direct bearing on the theme of the day. In this case the central idea is *The Passages*

41

the *Akedah,* the binding of Isaac. The reading on the first day tells the story of the birth of Isaac: "And the Lord remembered Sarah as He had said, and the Lord did unto Sarah as He had spoken." According to tradition Sarah was "remembered" on Rosh Ha-Shanah, as were the Matriarch Rachel and Hannah (see page 45). The birth of Isaac, too, took place on Rosh Ha-Shanah. Therefore, although the following passages are seemingly unconnected with Rosh Ha-Shanah, the opening paragraph has, according to the Midrash, a direct bearing on the festival, quite apart from the fact, that it leads up to the portion read on the next day.

Various homiletical attempts have been made to connect the Torah reading with the significance of the festival.

Besides the birth of Isaac, the Torah reading also relates how Hagar, Abraham's secondary wife, was driven out because Sarah found her son, Ishmael, unworthy to grow up together with Isaac. Abraham objected, but God intervened and ordered him to do as Sarah demanded. When Hagar gave up hope of survival in the desert and laid the weeping child down to die, an angel called to her and informed her that God had heard the cry of the boy "where he is". According to the Midrash, the angels came to God, and demanded to know why Ishmael, whose descendants would cause Israel such harm, should not be left to die. God justified the salvation of Ishmael "where he is", for at that moment he did not deserve to die. The future deeds of his descendants could not influence his present fate. On Rosh Ha-Shanah, man is judged by his present state. Even if afterwards he is unable to live up to his good resolutions, it is by his present repentance, and by his present firm resolution that he is judged.

On the second day of Rosh Ha-Shanah the *Akedah* story is read. Here, the message is quite clear and also serves as a major theme in the liturgy and the *shofar* blowing. Abraham's faith

"Hagar in the Wilderness" by Jean Baptiste Camille Corot, 1835.

stood the test and ensured the survival of his progeny down the ages. For, as frequently pointed out by the sages, reward and punishment are mostly in kind. Abraham was prepared to destroy the bearer of his destiny. His reward is the everlasting survival of the people he fathered.

On each day, two Torah scrolls are taken out of the ark. The first is for the passages described above. From the second, the special sacrifices of Rosh Ha-Shanah are read. These consist of the specific sacrifices of the day as well as the daily offering and the offerings for the *Rosh Ḥodesh;* for Rosh Ha-Shanah is at the same time *Rosh Hodesh.* *Maftir*

Following the Torah reading, the *haftarah* is read from the Prophets. The custom of reading from the Prophets on Shabbat *The Prophetical Readings*

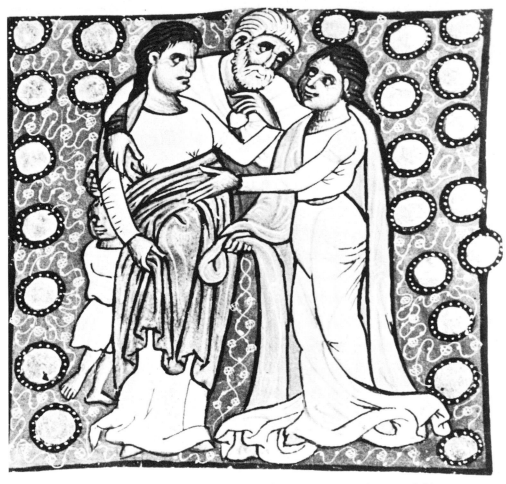

Elkanah with his two wives, Hannah and Penina. Hannah, who was child-less, prayed for a child. The child, she promised, would serve God all the days of its life. Her prayers were answered, according to tradition, on Rosh Ha-Shanah, and she gave birth to the Prophet Samuel. This portion of the Bible is read on Rosh Ha-Shanah both because of its traditional dating and because it emphasizes the power of prayer in determining destiny. From the *Conradin Bible*, Southern Italy, 13th century.

44

and the festivals probably originated in the times when Torah readings were forbidden, so that a portion was read from the Prophets which would prove a reminder of the Torah portion. On the first day of Rosh Ha-Shanah the first chapter of Samuel is read. This is a description of the prophet Samuel's birth. Hannah, his mother, was barren and was remembered on Rosh Ha-Shanah. The portion concludes with her prayer of praise and gratitude.

The *haftarah* on the second day is taken from Jeremiah, the prophet of doom, and is one of the few chapters in that book which speak of hope. It is a description of the redemption to come, when Israel will return to its land. It concludes with the promise: "Is Ephraim a darling son unto me? Is he a child that is dandled? For as often as I speak of him, I do earnestly remember him still: Therefore my heart yearneth for him, I will surely have compassion upon him, saith the Lord."

3.   TEN DAYS OF PENITENCE
Return Unto Me And I Will Return Unto You

Their Meaning

The Ten Days of Penitence are counted from Rosh Ha-Shanah, the first day of Tishrei, till Yom Kippur, the tenth day of Tishrei. Nevertheless, the term often refers only to the seven intermediate days which link the two festivals. The heightened spiritual awareness left by Rosh Ha-Shanah should continue to influence a person as he returns to his daily routine. The resolutions, made in a moment of spiritual fervor, have, in the period following Rosh Ha-Shanah, to meet the challenge of everyday life. At the same time, the Ten Days are a preparation for the Day of Atonement. No man is beyond sin: "For there is not a righteous man upon earth, that doeth good, and sinneth not."

Each person should see himself as belonging to that category whose judgement is held in abeyance, as they are neither wholly good, nor yet wholly bad (see page 34). Accordingly, during the period of the Ten Days, he should make every effort to attain forgiveness. Good deeds are not sufficient because, although figuratively speaking, they add to the present balance, they do not affect the debit account accumulated during the past year. To pay that account a person must repent, and the opportunity for repentance is given by the Ten Days. This is the major aspect of those days and explains why they are called the Ten Days of Penitence. The sages advise a person to repent the day before his death; which, since no-one knows when he will die, means every day. It is, however, during the Ten Days, that God, so to say, makes it easier for a person to repent and that repentance is more easily accepted. To this concept the verse from Isaiah was applied: "Seek ye the Lord while He may be found, Call ye upon Him while He is near."

Application

It is, therefore, customary during the Ten Days to apply the *halakhah* more strictly, and where there is a divergence of opinion, to follow the more stringent ruling. Halakhic strictness with oneself should be accompanied by special attention to social behavior. Consideration for others is essential for man's relationship with God.

Seliḥot are still recited in the morning until Yom Kippur, and special insertions are made in the *Amidah,* stressing God's role as King and Judge, and beseeching Him to remember man favorably and grant him continued life. In the morning and afternoon (*Minḥah*) the special *"Avinu Malkenu"* ("Our Father, our King . . .") prayer is recited. At one time it was customary to fast during the whole of the Ten Days, eating only in the evenings.

Such customs, obviously, intensify the atmosphere of repentance as the Jew prepares himself for the Day of Atonement.

Fast of Gedaliah

Of the seven intermediate days three are prominent: the Fast of Gedaliah, *Shabbat Shuvah* and *erev* Yom Kippur. The death of Gedaliah (see page 6) has been compared in its significance and tragic consequences to the destruction of the Temple. It was ordained as a public fast day, and was already mentioned as such in the Bible, where Zechariah called it "the fast of the seventh (month)". Although the murder was committed on the first of Tishrei, the fast was postponed to the day following Rosh Ha-Shanah, as it is forbidden to fast or mourn on a festival. Should the next day be a Sabbath, the fast is again postponed to Sunday.

Shabbat Shuvah

The Sabbath of the seven days is called either *Shabbat Shuvah* or *Shabbat Teshuvah*. Certain Sabbath days during the year have a

The rabbi's sermon on *Shabbat Shuvah*, depicted in the *Venice Minhagim Book* (a book of customs), 1601.

47

special name, usually taken from the *haftarah* read on that day. In this case the *haftarah* begins with the words *Shuvah Yisrael,* "Return, O Israel, unto the Lord thy God . . ." and the first word gives the Sabbath its name. Alternatively, the Sabbath is called *Shabbat Teshuvah* since both the *haftarah* and the Ten Day period call for repentance (= *teshuvah*).

Although today, in most congregations in the Diaspora, it is *The Sermon* customary for the rabbi or minister to give a sermon every Sabbath, it was originally considered the rabbi's task only twice a year: on the Sabbath preceding Passover (*Shabbat Ha-Gadol,* the "Great Sabbath") and on *Shabbat Shuvah.* On the latter day the rabbi is expected to speak on the significance of the High Holy Days to arouse the congregation to repentance and good deeds.

Erev Yom Kippur

The day preceding Yom Kippur is regarded as a semi-festival, A Semi-Festival which is usually spent in making preparations for the Day of Atonement. In most rites the *seliḥot* are extremely short, for there is much to be done before the beginning of the Holy Day. The sages taught that eating on *erev* Yom Kippur is considered as meritorious as fasting on Yom Kippur itself, and carries the same reward. Like the fasting, the eating must be for the sake of the commandment and not out of gluttony. In this way, the meals on *erev* Yom Kippur become sanctified.

An illustration in a German book on Jewish belief, depicting the *Kapparot* ceremony and the festive meal before the Day of Atonement (opposite). The *Kapparot* ceremony (below).

The *Kapparot* ceremony by J.D. Kirszenbaum (1900-1954).

Kapparot is a widespread custom which takes place immedi- ately after the morning service, often before breakfast. This is a substitute ritual in which the celebrant waves a fowl around his head, while at the same time reciting the verse three times: "This is my substitute, this is my exchange, this is my atonement; this fowl will go to its death, and I shall enter a good and long life and peace."

The ceremony is symbolic and reminiscent of the Temple sacrifices. One of the ideas behind the atonement sacrifice in the Temple is that guilt is transferred to the sacrificial animal which pays the penalty for the man's sin, while the person is cleansed. Through the offering of the animal, the person should be brought to the realization that it is he who should in reality be paying the penalty.

After the brief ceremony, the chicken is "redeemed" by money which is given to the poor, and immediately slaughtered to be eaten for the meal preceding the fast. Alternatively, the chicken is left unredeemed and given to the poor. Its intestines are thrown away in a place where the birds can eat them.

The *Kapparot* ceremony is sometimes carried out with a fish or even just with money. It has become widely popular, but many distinguished rabbinical authorities opposed it as being a heathen custom with magic implications.

Another custom found frequently is that of visiting the graves of parents and members of the family on *erev* Yom Kippur.

Before the afternoon service (*Minḥah*), which is held early on *erev* Yom Kippur, it is customary to immerse oneself in the ritual bath for the sake of purity, and dress in Sabbath clothes. Collection plates for charity are frequently laid out in the synagogue to receive donations or the money from the *kapparot*. The *Amidah* is that of normal weekdays, but, at its conclusion, the confessional *Al-Het* prayer is added. Although it is not yet Yom Kippur, the confessional prayer conveys the atmosphere of the holy day. The sages thought it proper that a person confess his sins before the concluding meal, in the case of a last-minute mishap.

A custom seldom seen nowadays is to receive "lashes" *Lashes* (*malkot*). At one time lashes were a common form of punishment by the communal authorities. On *erev* Yom Kippur they are purely symbolic. Token blows, usually with a leather strap, are administered lightly; the penitent recites the short confessional (*Ashamnu*) and the striker of the blows recites, "For He is merciful and forgives iniquity."

Strap from Kurdistan, 19th century, used for the "lashes" on the eve of the Day of Atonement. Note the inscription at the bottom: "Atonement for sins; forgiveness for iniquities; pardon for transgressions."

Following the afternoon service the main meal of the day is *The Meal* eaten. This immediately precedes the fast. The meal is both festive and solemn and should include both meat and wine. It should not, however, be a heavy meal, but a preparation for the coming fast. Often chicken is served, frequently the fowl which was used for *kapparot* in the morning. The meal finishes before sunset because the fast of Yom Kippur is from "eve to eve", and like the Sabbath, is extended slightly so that it begins early, well before sunset, and terminates the next day after dark. Many parents bless their children before leaving for the synagogue.

52

The Spirit of the Day

Yom Kippur, the Day of Atonement, is the most solemn day of *Atonement*
the Jewish year and is the climax to the Days of Awe. It is the
day on which the Jew as an individual, and the nation as a whole,
are cleansed of their sins and granted atonement. The concept
that man can achieve atonement for his sins is basic to Judaism.
Man is a dynamic organism, who has free choice to do good or
evil, but even having committed evil he can regain his former
purity through atonement. Judaism sees life as a sort of ladder.

Belt and buckle worn on the Day of Atonement. The buckle carries the
inscription, "For this day shall atonement be made for you, to cleanse
you; from all your sins shall you be clean before the Lord" (Leviticus 16:30).
Poland, 18th-19th century.

Man either goes up or down, but is never stationary. With each good deed he raises himself to a higher spiritual level and with each evil one he sinks lower. Yom Kippur adds a new dimension: however low man has fallen he can pull himself up again. Yom Kippur is a day "unto you", for man, of which he stands in urgent need in order to become reconciled to God, and, which God has made available to man for his own sake.

The Midrash illustrates the point in its own picturesque fashion: Wisdom was asked, "What is the punishment of the sinner? " It answered, "Evil will persecute the sinners." Prophecy was asked the same question and answered, "The soul that sinneth, it shall die." The Torah was asked. It replied, "If he brings a sin-offering, he will be atoned for." When God was asked, He said, "Let him repent and his sin shall be atoned." The idea is further embellished by a homily on the verse of the Bible: "At the mouth of two witnesses, or three witnesses, shall he that is to die be put to death; at the mouth of one witness he shall not be put to death." Wisdom and Prophecy would condemn the sinner to death. So would the Torah, if the sinner cannot find a sacrifice. Only the one witness — God — will not condemn him if he repents, for God has made atonement possible.

The concept of atonement is found in other religions as well. Unique to Judaism, of all the world's great faiths, is the setting aside of a specific day for this purpose. The Bible calls the day *Shabbat Shabbaton,* a Sabbath of Sabbaths. It is not just a memory of the world's creation but a memory of Creation itself. Man, the pinnacle of God's Creation, for whom everything else was created, stands newly created after having received atonement. According to Rabbi Judah ha-Nasi, the compiler of the Mishnah, the power of Yom Kippur is such that the day itself automatically atones for man without any further requirements on man's part. The other sages disagreed. Only if a person repents

54

"The Eve of Yom Kippur" by Moritz Oppenheim. Note the postures of repentence and the white robes.

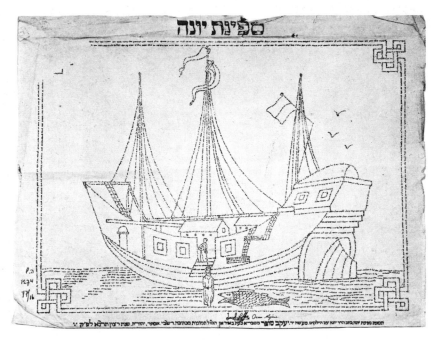

The Book of Jonah, done in micography, showing the boat, the whale and Jonah. Tiberias, 1891. The illustration contains the whole text of the book.

of his sin is he granted atonement on Yom Kippur. Even then, there are additional stages in the case of extreme transgressions until full atonement is attained. Those transgressions in the Bible which carry either a death penalty or extirpation *(karet)* are finally atoned for only by suffering, and if the defamation of God's name (*ḥillul ha-Shem*) is involved, only death itself provides final atonement. Nevertheless, in each case, Yom Kippur, coupled with repentance, provides an important stage in the process.

Repentance is a vital factor in attaining atonement. The Bible frequently mentions repentance, and it is a major theme in the prophetical writings. A complete book, Jonah, whose message is

Repentance

56

Jonah, from a 15th century Spanish translation of the Bible. Madrid, Escorial.

God's acceptance of man's penitence, is included in the Scriptures. The possibility of repentance is open to every man, at all times: "and as for the wickedness of the wicked, he shall not stumble thereby on the day he turneth from his wickedness."

Page from a handwritten Italian *maḥzor* for Rosh Ha-Shanah. In the center of the page is the beginning of the *Amidah* with the *Zokhrenu le-Ḥayyim* prayer. Around the sides is a commentary to that prayer.

Simeon bar Yoḥai (2nd century c.e.), explained the meaning of the verse as proving that even a totally wicked person who lives his whole life in sin is forgiven the moment he truly repents. Yaakov ben Korshai (2nd century c.e.), stated that one hour of repentance and good deeds in this world is better than the whole life of the world to come. In certain cases, however, the possibility of repentance is withheld, such as for one who causes others to sin, or for the person who deliberately sins, relying on Yom Kippur to atone for him.

True repentance consists of three major steps: regret for the past; resolution not to repeat the sin in the future, and confession. Public sins and sins against others should be confessed publicly; private sins should be confessed directly before God. The sages pointed out that the proof of true repentance becomes evident only if the sinner refrains from repeating his sin when the opportunity presents itself under exactly similar circumstances. An important proviso is that the person's abstention is due to contrition and not to fear of punishment or physical weakness. Despite repentance and confession, a person continues to confess his sin every year on Yom Kippur, as remorse never leaves him.

The sages also divided repentance into two or even three categories: repentance through suffering; repentance out of fear, and repentance out of love for God, the last being of the highest merit. Repentance not only absolves a person from sin; it even adds to his credit. He who repents out of fear has all his deliberate sins counted as unwitting ones. He who repents out of love for God, however, has his sins counted as good deeds (*mitzvot*). The sages discuss the relative worth of a penitent sinner and a saint who has never sinned, and conclude that the former stands on a higher plane. The sinner, who has experienced sin and comes to realize its true significance, is filled with remorse through which he rises to heights which the saint cannot attain, being ignorant of one of the dimensions of the human spirit. The latter is like a person who has never experienced darkness, and therefore, cannot fully appreciate light. Remorse and penitence give a person a new understanding of God through which he reaches atonement.

For one type of sin no amount of remorse will help; the sin of one man against his fellow. In the case where damage has been inflicted, it must first be repaired. Even after making amends, God will not forgive until forgiveness has been obtained from the injured party. If the injured party refuses to forgive, the offender is required to apologize in front of three witnesses. If, after three such efforts, the injured party still refuses to forgive, the offender is absolved, unless the injured party is his teacher when no number of times is sufficient. If the injured party is dead, then confession must be made at his grave in front of ten witnesses. The importance of obtaining forgiveness from one's fellows has given rise to a picturesque custom. Before the opening service on Yom Kippur eve, congregants ask each other for forgiveness for any wrongs done intentionally or unintentionally during the past year. Having made one's peace with one's fellows, a person is ready to seek forgiveness from God.

Yom Kippur is a very personal experience in which each man *National* wrestles with his own conscience. But its importance lies also in *Atonement* the national sphere. This is obvious from the Yom Kippur Temple service, where the High Priest acted as representative of the whole people, and a great part of the atonement service was for the nation as a whole. Today, too, the confessional prayers are conducted in the plural form thereby including all Israel. Traditionally, Yom Kippur is the day on which Moses came down from Mount Sinai with the second two tablets of stone, after obtaining God's forgiveness for Israel's sin with the Golden Calf. This day was set aside for generations to come as a day of forgiveness for the Jewish people. The sages also relate how in the Second Temple period it was customary to tie some red wool to the Temple gate which would turn white as a sign that the people had found forgiveness. Yom Kippur, with its strong overtones of personal atonement for sins and transgressions, is at the same time a day of national cleansing when the Jewish people as a whole regains its purity.

Apart from the description of the Yom Kippur ceremony in *In Ancient* Leviticus, there is no information in the Bible as to how the day *Times*

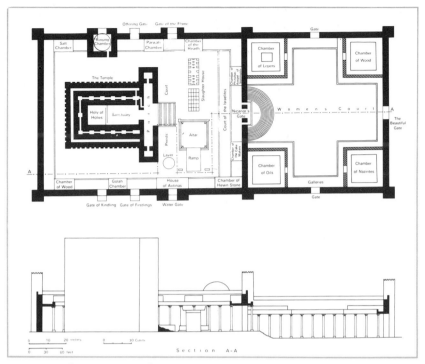

Suggested restoration of the Second Temple, according to the Mishnah *Middot* and Josephus' *Jewish Antiquities*.

was observed prior to the Babylonian exile. It seems that in the year Solomon built the Temple, observance of the Day of Atonement was waived and the people celebrated the consecration of the Temple with food, drink, and festivities. A detailed description of the atonement service in the Second Temple period is found in the Mishnah, where seven out of the eight chapters of Tractate Yoma deal with the High Priest's Temple service.

Ben Sira (Ecclesiasticus) who lived at the beginning of the second century b.c.e. gives a lyric account of the High Priest on Yom Kippur. He also mentions that the people prayed as the

High Priest offering incense on the altar. Copperplate engraving of a Hebrew-Latin edition of the Mishnah, Amsterdam, 1700-1704.

High Priest brought the sacrifices. A much fuller description is given by Philo, the Jewish Hellenistic philosopher who lived in Alexandria towards the end of the Second Temple period. "The holy day is entirely devoted to prayers and supplications, and men from morn to eve employ their leisure in nothing else but offering petitions of humble entreaty ... for remission of their sins, voluntary and involuntary, and entertain bright hopes looking not to their own merits but to the gracious nature of Him, Who sets pardon before chastisement."

סדר

עבורת יום הכפורים

כנהגים לומר

כבית הכנסת שלישי

ספרדי בעיר

טריאסטי

יע''א

הובא לבית הרפוס על ידי הצעיר

שמואל אשכנזי יצ''ו

היושב בעיר תל''ל

וויניציאה

בשנת נדרשה א''ה ח''

לפ''ק

63

Yom Kippur *maḥzor* according to the Sephardi rite for the city of Trieste.
Printed in Venice, 1799.

Evidently those Jews who could not go up to Jerusalem attended the synagogue all day much as is done today. Fragments of an order of prayer for the Day of Atonement have also been found in one of the two Qumran caves belonging to the Dead Sea sectarians. It is remarkable how little the content and theme of Yom Kippur has changed from Philo's days, some 2,000 years ago, when the Temple was still standing: "On the tenth day is the fast which is carefully observed not only by the zealous for piety and holiness but also by those who never act religiously in the rest of their life ... the worse vie with the better in self-denial and virtue. The high dignity of this day has two aspects, one as a festival, the other as a time for purification and escape from sins for which indemnity is granted by the bounties of the gracious God, Who has given to repentance the same honor as to innocence from sin."

There is a famous description by Rabbi Simeon ben Gamaliel of Yom Kippur and the fifteenth of Av which, he states, were the happiest two days of the year, when the maidens of Jerusalem would go forth, all dressed in white, and dance in the vineyards. They would call out to the young men to choose each man a wife for himself. The plain girls would say, "Set not your eyes on beauty", and the beautiful girls would say, "Set not your eyes on family lineage." Despite the repentance and abstinence practiced on Yom Kippur, it was never a sad day. Its atmosphere was solemn but this was always accompanied by the confidence and joy at finding atonement.

Illustrated page from *Kirchliche Verfassung* by Bodenschatz (1717-1797). The center illustration depicts the *Kol Nidrei* service, as the Torah Scrolls are being taken round the synagogue. The panels (clockwise from top left) show the administration of lashes; the "affliction" of going barefoot; visiting the cemetery; *Kapparot*; and giving charity.

Fig. VIII.   *Das Verſöhnungs Feſt.*

G. Eichler. inv. et del.   P. II.   G. P. Nußbiegel. sc.

Only in the Book of Jubilees (a Jewish sectarian work from approximately the 2nd century b.c.e.) do we find that Yom Kippur is connected with mourning. The day on which Jacob heard of Joseph's supposed death was the tenth of Tishrei, and, because of the grief caused Jacob, this day was ordained as a day for seeking atonement. The goat offered in the Temple as an atonement sacrifice (see page 88) is a reminder of the goat which Joseph's brothers slaughtered and sent to Jacob in order to deceive him after selling Joseph. This theme is found nowhere else and is certainly foreign to later rabbinic thought.

The Book of Jubilees also differs from tradition in its system *The Calendar* for reckoning the calendar. The question of the calendar was of vital importance for the unity of the nation and a variant reckoning resulted in the formation of diverging sects. The Dead Sea Sect probably also had a different calendar. This would explain the mysterious reference to Yom Kippur in the *Pesher Habbakuk* scroll where the Day of Atonement is termed "their Sabbath of rest".

> "... the Wicked Priest pursued after the Teacher of Righteousness to swallow him up in his fury, even to his place of exile, and on the occasion of the sacred season of rest, the Day of Atonement, appeared among them to swallow them up and to make them stumble on the fast day, their Sabbath of rest."

A unified calendar became one of the immediate tasks of the Jewish leadership after the destruction of the Second Temple. A serious clash on the question occurred during the time of Rabban Gamaliel (2nd century c.e.), when the leadership was still struggling to assert itself. Rabbi Joshua, one of the foremost sages of his day, refused to accept the evidence of witnesses with regard to the new moon for the month of Tishrei (see page 12) with the result that Rosh Ha-Shanah would fall a day later than the one fixed by Rabban Gamaliel. Rabban Gamaliel asserted the authority of his position as *Nasi* (President of the Sanhedrin) and forced Rabbi Joshua to come to him holding his stick and purse on the day which according to Rabbi Joshua's reckoning was the Day of Atonement. The other leading rabbis of the day, although they sympathized with Joshua's arguments, admitted that Gamaliel's authority had to be upheld.

Differences in calendar reckoning also cause a sharp division between traditional Jewish practice and that of the Samaritans and Karaites. The former celebrate only one day of Rosh Ha-Shanah. On Yom Kippur, which is frequently as much as a month different from the Jewish date, they fast from eve to eve and spend the day in prayer, continuous reading of the Pentateuch and *piyyutim.* Every member of the community over the age of one must fast. The Karaite calendar permits Rosh Ha-Shanah to be on any day of the week (as opposed to the tradition that the first day of Rosh Ha-Shanah cannot fall on a Sunday, Wednesday or Friday). As a result, the Karaite Yom Kippur, too, can fall on days avoided by the traditional Jewish calendar.

Reciting *seliḥot* in the synagogue during the penitential season.

Liturgy

The evening prayers of Yom Kippur begin early, and continue till dark. They are probably the best known in all Jewish liturgy. Many a Jew, who has lost all contact with Judaism, will nevertheless attend the *Kol Nidrei* service on Yom Kippur eve. A famous case is that of Franz Rosenzweig, who later became a leading modern Jewish religious philosopher. Rosenzweig had already decided on baptism when he attended the *Kol Nidrei* service as a last experience of Judaism. He left the service a changed man and from then on searched for his roots in the past of the Jewish people and its intellectual heritage. It is difficult to pinpoint exactly what it is that is so moving in the evening service. It seems to be a combination of several elements; the prayers and the special melodies, but even more, the atmosphere engendered by the entrance of the most holy day of the year, and the call to repentance that pervades the synagogue. This is enhanced by the mounting tension of the *ḥazzan* who begins quietly, almost in a whisper and finishes strongly with the whole congregation joining in.

The Evening Service

The service opens with Torah scrolls being taken out of the ark. Custom differs as to whether one, three, or all the scrolls are used. Many people go forward to kiss the scrolls as they are taken around the central *bimah*. Meanwhile the verse: "Light is sown for the righteous and gladness for the upright in heart" is recited. The *ḥazzan* then takes up his position with a leading member of the congregation on either side. These remain with him until the evening service proper. This is an allusion to Moses, who, when he prayed for Israel during their battle against the Amalekites, was accompanied by his brother Aaron and his nephew Hur, who supported his arms, which he held up to heaven.

The Opening of the Service

From the practical point of view, the reader with his two attendants have the outward appearance of a court of law, for

Jews taking the *more Judaico* oath. Note the Jewish badge on the left shoulder or arm. Woodcut, 1509.

which a minimum of three judges are necessary. This gives legal sanction to the recital which follows, which permits the congre-, gants to pray together with any transgressors. The declaration was first introduced by Meir of Rothenburg (1220–1293). Anyone in the community who had been excommunicated is not only allowed to return and join in the service, but is even welcomed. Their participation is seen as a sign of their repentance. Meir's innovation was necessary because in the Middle Ages the ban was often used as the community's most effective punishment.

The declaration, made in all solemnity at the beginning of the service, is in the spirit of the Talmud, which states that a fast day in which sinners do not participate is not effective. When the High Priest brought incense into the Holy of Holies in the Temple to atone for the people, one of the ingredients was galbanum, which itself has an unpleasant odor, but was nevertheless mixed together with the other spices. So, too, the sinner must be included in the Jewish community for although he has sinned he is still an integral part of Israel.

After the declaration, the reader begins to chant *Kol Nidrei* *Kol Nidrei* which is a declaration of annulment of vows and oaths. It is recited three times. The recital is supposed to last until night, when the evening service proper can begin. The haunting melody is basically the same in most Ashkenazi communities and is believed to be of great antiquity. It is begun quietly as if the reader and congregation were amazed and awed at entering the palace of the King, only gradually gathering confidence as they find that God is not only King but also a merciful Father.

Kol Nidrei is not directly connected with Yom Kippur. Only because the fear of unconsciously transgressing a vow was so great was *Kol Nidrei* included. In most communities it is recited in Aramaic, although certain rites have a Hebrew version. Yet, although *Kol Nidrei* is today the traditional liturgy for Yom

Musical notations for the *Kol Nidrei* service. The same tune is used virtually the world over.

Kippur eve, there was great opposition to its inclusion in the service, from its very inception. According to Rashi (Rabbi Shlomo Itzhaki, France, 1040 – 1105), *Kol Nidrei* was instituted by the *Geonim* (the Babylonian sages, heads of the academies in the early Middle Ages, c. 600–1100). In geonic literature, however, there are many who voiced their opposition, for oaths once made cannot be automatically annulled by declaration.

Kol Nidrei is first mentioned by Yehudai Gaon (8th century) who relates that the custom of reciting *Kol Nidrei* arose "in other lands", and was not kept in Babylon. Amram Gaon (9th century), author of the first compilation of the prayers, called it "a foolish custom", and Natronai and Hai bar Naḥshon (9th century) also opposed the custom. Only Sa'adiah (10th century) supported it. The opposition to *Kol Nidrei* continued after the geonic period, and many leading rabbis either ommited all mention of *Kol Nidrei* or wrote against the custom. *Kol Nidrei* was never accepted in Catalonia or Algeria, and in Spain, under the influence of the Babylonian center, the *Kol Nidrei* was not included in the service. In Provence, the great Jewish center in southern France in the Middle Ages, *Kol Nidrei* was included for a time in the 12th century but was later abolished.

In Northern and Central Europe, the custom became generally established after Meir ben Samuel (11/12th century), the son-in-law of Rashi, changed the wording so as to refer to vows made in the coming year instead of in the past year. The Italian and Sephardi rites, however, retain the original form.

Kol Nidrei also gave rise to serious anti-semitic accusations against the Jews. It was claimed that Jewish oaths were worthless, as the Jews annuled all their oaths on the Day of Atonement. In the Disputation of Paris (1240), the apostate Nicholas Donin used the custom as proof of the perfidy of the Jews. In modern times as well, anti-Semites such as Buxtorf and Eisen-

An open "gateway" from the prayer, "He Who opens the gate of mercy for us . . .",
of the prayers for Yom Kippur in the *Worms Mahzor,* Germany, late 13th century.
According to tradition, the gates of heaven open on the eve of the Day of Atonement
to receive the prayers of every Jew, and it is on this night that the Almighty makes
his decision as to who will live and who will die in the coming year. The gates are
closed at the termination of the day. In most 13th and 14th century *mahzorim* from
southern Germany, the prayer is illustrated by a gateway, sometimes with the addition
of a pair of gates standing open. The buildings above the gateway presumably depict
the heavenly Jerusalem.

Various *shofarot* used through the ages:
1) Perleburg, Germany, 1726, inscribed with a quotation from Isaiah 27:13.
2) Venice, 17th century. 3) Pitigliano, Italy, 17th century. 4) Trieste, 17th century. 5) Rome, 17th century.
Silver *maḥzor* binding, Galicia, early 19th century. One panel depicts a scene of the *Akedah,* the Binding of Isaac. The other panel depicts Jacob's dream of the angels ascending and descending the heavenly ladder.

menger made similar charges. In the Middle Ages, a special "Jew's oath", *more Judaico,* was instituted to counteract the "effect" of *Kol Nidrei.* In modern times, especially in Russia, the *Kol Nidrei* prayer proved to be ammunition for the opponents of Jewish emancipation. As from 1860, a special introduction was printed in Russian prayer books explaining that *Kol Nidrei* did not apply to oaths made in a court of law. The fact is that *Kol Nidrei* applies only to personal religious vows which do not affect any other person. Nor has it any bearing on an oath imposed by law. However, the Reform movement in Germany recommended the abolition of the custom when it gathered for the Brunswick Synod in 1844. It was replaced by psalms or prayers, sung to the original melody. Only in 1961 did the Reform Union Prayer Book of the United States re-institute the complete text.

Yom Kippur services in Verdun, France, during World War II.

After *Kol Nidrei* several biblical verses referring to God's
atonement for Israel are recited by the reader and the congregation and this is followed by the *she-heḥeyanu* benediction (see
page 19), which is recited on every festival. Women who have
already recited the *she-heḥeyanu* when lighting candles do not
repeat the benediction but only answer "Amen".

When the *Shema* prayer is recited during the evening service,
and again on the following day, the verse, "Blessed be His glorious
sovereign Name for ever and ever," is said aloud. This verse,
which does not appear in the biblical text of the *Shema*, was
inserted by the sages and is said very softly all the year round. On
Yom Kippur, however, it is recited aloud. The Midrash has it that
Moses heard the angels reciting this verse when he went up on
Mount Sinai, and introduced it into the *Shema*. Since it was the
prayer of the angels, it was to be said silently so as not to arouse
their antagonism; on Yom Kippur, however, when man reaches
the heights of the ministering angels, it is said aloud.

At the end of the *Amidah,* the two confessional prayers
Ashamnu and *Al-Ḥet* are added. They have previously been said
in the afternoon service. During the Yom Kippur services the
"short confessional", *Ashamnu,* is repeated ten times and the
"long confessional". *Al-Ḥet,* which is not recited in the special
Ne'ilah service, eight times. Each of the regular *amidot* closes
with these two confessionals and they are again recited with the
following *selihot,* or in the reader's repetition. Both confessionals
date back at least to geonic times and probably originated in the
fourth or fifth centuries. They are alphabetic acrostics and describe sins in general. They are couched in the plural form ("For
the sin which we have sinned . . ."), thus clearly supporting
communal responsibility. The various rites have different versions
of the *Al-Ḥet* prayer. The Ashkenazi form contains two sins for
every letter of the alphabet, with a further list added according

"Ashamnu", drawing by Alphonse Levy (1843-1918).

75

to the punishment. The Reform rite has a shortened version. Many communities sing the *Al-Ḥet* prayer, or at least the refrain. A ḥasidic tale tells how the Ba'al Shem Tov once arrived at a town where he was informed that the rabbi sang the *Al-Ḥet* to a joyous tune. When the Ba'al Shem Tov asked him about it he replied that the servant who really loved his master found joy in sweeping out all the dirt from his master's stables, and would sing out of sheer happiness at being able to serve his master in this way.

The *Ashamnu* confession, so called after its first word, is made up of twenty five words of which the initial letters form an alphabetical acrostic, some of the letters are repeated. Each word represents a sinful activity: "we have sinned, we have acted treacherously . . .", etc. It is customary to smite one's breast at the recitation of each sin in both the confessionals.

In each of the services on Yom Kippur, *piyyutim* and *selihot* are recited but these differ according to rite. There are also differences between communities, some including more and others fewer *piyyutim.* Certain rabbis, such as Menahem Ha-Meiri (1249—1315), opposed the recitation of *piyyutim* altogether and preferred sermons on repentance in their stead.

The Torah reading which follows the morning service is from Leviticus, and is a description of the Tabernacle-Temple service on the Day of Atonement. For the *haftarah,* a description of the ideal fast is read from Isaiah. During the afternoon *(Minḥah)* service the reading is also from Leviticus and deals with forbidden marriages. It is in fact, practically a continuation of the morning reading, which is probably the reason for choosing this particular chapter. Moralists point out that when man reaches the highest spiritual heights he has to be reminded of basic moral tenets. For when man is carried away by high spiritual ideals, he occasionally tends to forget elementary rights and wrongs.

The Torah Readings

Page from prayer book written in Florence in 1492. The panel begins the *selihot* section and has decorated border with floral, human and animal motifs.

As on other fast days, the *Minḥah* Torah reading is accompanied by a *haftarah*. On Yom Kippur this consists of the Book of Jonah which relates Jonah's mission to Nineveh, the capital of Assyria, to warn the city of its impending destruction because of its misdeeds. The story divides naturally into three parts: how Jonah tried to avoid undertaking the mission; how he warned Nineveh and the result of his warning, and the effect on Jonah when God pardoned the city. Each of these sections, while having no relevance to the Torah reading, has a direct message for Yom Kippur. In the first part, Jonah tries to escape from his destiny but cannot. The second part demonstrates the efficacy of

"In the Synagogue Courtyard on Yom Kippur", drawing by Alphonse Levy.

repentance. Nineveh's inhabitants with the king in the lead, repent of their past and God relents. The city is saved. The third section shows how God explains the workings of His providence to Jonah. God demonstrates to him His love for his creatures, whose lives are dear to Him. The people of Nineveh are judged not by their past, nor yet — according to the Midrash — by their future destruction of Israel, — but by their present. Their present penitence earns them salvation.

In Hebrew the name of the festival used in the Bible, *Yom Ha-Kippurim* has the plural form, the Day of Atonements. This, the rabbis explain, is not only because the living receive atonement, but also the dead. A dogma of Judaism is belief in an afterlife, when the soul continues to live, and is also liable to punishment for the sins it committed on earth. The idea that the living can seek atonement for the dead is found in literary sources as early as the Book of Maccabees (c. 2nd century b.c.e.). There, Judah and his men pray for their fallen comrades and bring offerings to the Temple to atone for their sins. It is also found frequently in rabbinic literature, although certain *geonim,* such as Hai and his pupil Nissim ben Jacob (11th century) believed that the soul is judged on its own merit and nothing the living can do will affect the dead. The custom of saying prayers and donating charity for the dead was widely accepted, and became increasingly popular. The *Yizkor* service is one of the best attended services in the synagogue by both men and women. Historically, it gained special prominence after the Rhineland massacres which took place during the First Crusade when the *Av ha-Rahamim* prayer was introduced.

The *Yizkor* ceremony was originally held only on Yom Kippur, but was afterwards introduced on the last day of Pesaḥ, on Shavuot and on Shemini Aẓeret. It is so named because of the opening word *Yizkor* "May (God) Remember . . .". It is a prayer

The Yizkor Remembrance Service

79

for the departed, and the names of the dead are read out. At the same time charity is promised and the donor beseeches God that by virtue of his charity, the souls may enjoy eternal life in God's presence.

In most synagogues, those whose parents are still alive do not participate in the ceremony but leave the synagogue in order to avoid the "evil eye", and because such a person might join in by mistake and say the remembrance prayer for his parents. It is also not considered right that a section of the congregation should remain idle during the service. Those whose parent has been dead

The Rosh Ha-Shanah service in an 18th century German synagogue Note the custom to open the ark for the *shofar* blowing. Copper engraving, 1734.

less than a year do not participate as their grief is still too fresh and their sorrow too great; mourning is not permitted on the festival and in their grief they might also disturb others. At the conclusion of the *Yizkor* service, the *Av ha-Raḥamim* prayer is recited in Ashkenazi communities for all those Jews martyred for their faith, and the whole congregation participate in this prayer. Today, special prayers for those that died in the Holocaust and for the soldiers who fell in the defense of the State of Israel are commonly recited.

Blessing the new moon at the termination of the Yom Kippur service. The top insert shows the Yom Kippur service while it is yet in progress. Germany, 1734.

The text of the *Yizkor* prayers differ from community to community and according to rite. The Sephardi prayer, which is called *Ashkavah*, forms a part of the evening service on Yom Kippur eve before *Ma'ariv*. The vows for charity are, however, made the following day prior to the afternoon service.

In the Conservative rite, introductory readings and appropriate verses from the Psalms are added both in Hebrew and in the vernacular. The Reform synagogues have partially abolished the custom and recite *Yizkor* only on Yom Kippur before *Ne'ilah* and on the last day of Passover. The traditional text is shortened and Psalm 23 is added together with readings from poets of the Middle Ages such as Judah Halevy and Ibn Gabirol. The ceremony is accompanied by solemn music and is concluded by the whole community reciting the *Kaddish* prayer.

The Riga synagogue during Rosh Ha-Shanah services, 1967. The curtain on the ark is white and the *ḥazzan* is surrounded by his choir.

The *Musaf* ("additional") prayer represents the additional sacrificial service in the Temple peculiar to that festival. On Yom Kippur this is a special occasion as it was the only day of the year that the High Priest entered the Holy of Holies. The silent *Amidah* follows the regular pattern of *Musaf* services with the confessional prayers added at the end. It is in the reader's repetition that the most notable prayers are included. These are a series of *piyyutim* of which the principle section is a description of the Temple service by the High Priest on Yom Kippur. This service is basically set out in the Bible reading of the day, and is more fully described in the Mishnah. The *piyyutim* are a poetic description based on the Mishnah. Originally the description of the Temple service was also recited during *Shaharit* and *Minhah* but during geonic times it became customary to recite the service only during *Musaf*.

Floor mosaic at the Bet-Shean synagogue (6th century c.e.) depicting, among other symbols, the *shofar*.

Although the High Priest could officiate whenever he wished, on Yom Kippur it was statutory for him to do so, and for seven days beforehand he lived in the Temple precincts in order to prepare himself for the Yom Kippur ritual. The service on Yom Kippur itself was of two kinds, the regular everyday service and the specific Yom Kippur service. For the former, the High Priest

Rosh Ha-Shanah — Yom Kippur *maḥzor* printed in Sulzbach, Germany in 1721 and bound in this silver binding in 1726. On the front (right) cover, Aaron and Moses are separated by the Burning Bush and on the back (left) cover is the *Akedah* ("Binding of Isaac").

Buying New Years greeting cards at a street stall (right). The festive meal prior to the Day of Atonement (below).

85

wore his normal priestly garments ornamented with gold, but for the latter he wore white. Gold evokes the memory of the Golden Calf; this is also a reason why women do not usually wear gold ornaments on Yom Kippur. Several times during the day the High Priest had to change his clothes, from gold to white and back again, and everytime he did this, as well as at the beginning of the day's service, he would sanctify himself by a ritual immersion.

One of the principal parts of the special atonement service in the Temple consisted of prayers recited by the High Priest over the sacrificial animals. During these prayers, the High Priest would utter the Holy Name, the Tetragrammaton. Three times the High Priest recited these atonement prayers, and in each of these prayers he pronounced the Tetragrammaton three times. The first prayer was recited when he placed his hands on the head of the bullock and prayed for atonement for himself and his family. Later he again used the same bullock and this time included in his prayer the priests, descendants of Aaron. The third prayer requested atonement for the whole people. For this prayer the *Azazel* goat was used.

The order of atonement is not accidental, nor does it denote self interest. Before the High Priest can become the peoples' representative in their atonement he has first to be utterly free from sin himself. Similarly, the priests, who helped with the service, had to be atoned for before it was possible to seek atonement for the people as a whole.

The *Azazel* goat was one of a pair, alike in all respects, for which the High Priest drew two lots. On one was written, "A sin-offering for the Lord" and on the other, "For *Azazel*." As the High Priest drew the lots he would raise the hand in which was the lot for a sin-offering and cry aloud, "A sin-offering for the Lord! " again using the Tetragrammaton. It was considered a

Depiction of the High Priest wearing the priestly garments.

Les Habits d'or du grand Prêtre.

good omen if the lot for sin-offering came up in the High Priest's right hand for right is symbolic of good and left of evil. Rabbinic tradition relates that one of the signs of impending doom was that for the 40 years prior to the destruction of the Temple, this lot always came up in the High Priest's left hand. The goat "for the Lord" was later slaughtered and its blood sprinkled before the Ark in the Holy of Holies. It was also used to atone for the altar.

Afterwards, the second goat, "For *Azazel*", was taken by the High Priest who rested his hands upon its head and recited the atonement prayer on behalf of all Israel. The goat, which now symbolically carried all of Israel's sins, was taken out to the Judean desert and pushed backwards over a high cliff to its destruction.

Neither the Bible nor the Mishnah explain the inner meaning of this ceremony. The Talmud explains the word *Azazel* to be related to *az*, strong. The goat is taken to a "strong", hard mountain. Another opinion sees a connection to two fallen angels who intermarried with "the daughters of men". Their names, Usa and Azael, are hinted at by the *Azazel* goat which atones for unchastity. In general, however, the Talmud accepts the ceremony as a divine commandment, not to be questioned, whose meaning is not divulged. Nevertheless, many commentators have explained the ceremony in different ways. Naḥmanides (1194–1270) describes the *Azazel* goat as an offering to the forces of evil, set aside by man at the command of God. Isaac Abrabanel regards the two goats as symbols of Jacob and Esau, the one turning to God and the other, spurning good, being condemned to the wasteland. This also fits the name of *Azazel* which is compounded of *az*, brazen and *azal*, Aramaic for "go, went." In the Septuagint, *Azazel* is translated as "the goat *(ez)* on which went the lot of dismissal *(azal)*."

Kapparot ceremony in Safed, 1972. A father is performing the ceremony over his son.

Kapparot is a substitute ritual in which the celebrant waves a fowl around his head.

Shofar maker, Haifa (above).
Yemenite Jew blowing
spiral *shofar* at the Western Wall,
Jerusalem (left).
Ashkenazi Jew blowing *shofar*
at the Western Wall, Jerusalem
(below).

The scapegoat being cast over the cliff, with the devil waiting below. Illustration from a 15th century German *mahzor*.

Every time the High Priest uttered the ineffable Name of God, the people gathered in the forecourt of the Temple would fall on their faces and say, "Blessed be His glorious sovereign Name for ever and ever." During the Yom Kippur service in the synagogue it is also customary to bow down when relating these events, with the knees and forehead touching the floor but with paper, cloth or *tallit* intervening. Only in the Temple was it permitted to prostrate oneself on the floor itself.

Another part of the Temple service recited in the synagogue is the description of the High Priest's entry into the inner sanctuary of the Temple, the Holy of Holies, with a special incense offering. On his exit as he stood in the outer·sanctuary, he recited a short prayer:

> "May it be Thy will, O Lord, our God and God of our fathers, that the coming year, if it be hot that it will be with plentiful rain, for us and all Israel wherever they are and let not the prayer of way farers be accepted when the world is in need of rain. May Your people Israel not need one another's help when earning a living, nor that of any other people. May no woman miscarry, and may the trees of the field yield their fruit. May sovereignty not be lost to the House of Judah."

The people waiting in the forecourt were unable to see the High Priest until he emerged from the outer sanctuary. They were understandably anxious, as it was believed that if the High Priest was unworthy he would not survive. This explains the brevity of the High Priest's prayer at the climax of the holy day's service. A ḥasidic saying, attributed to Israel of Rizhyn, gives a different explanation. When the High Priest entered the inner sanctuary and stood before the Divine Presence, he was lifted to the uttermost spiritual heights. Only when he again reached the "outside world" was he reminded of the material requirements of Israel. As these were now really minor matters he was brief with his prayers.

The High Priest entered the Holy of Holies two more times, to sprinkle the blood of the sacrifices. This he did once upwards and seven times downwards, each time counting; one, one and one, one and two . . . This too is recited in the synagogal service.

The series of *piyyutim* describing the Temple service is called the *Avodah* (service). There are different versions although they all follow the same general outline. The main section was composed at the latest, in the fourth century, but was enriched in the Middle Ages. The opening of the Piedmont rite was composed by Yose ben Yose, the earliest liturgical poet known by name (probably the 5th century c.e.), and gives a short account of biblical history, the creation of the world, the sinfulness of the early generations, the election of the Patriarchs and of Israel, up to the priestly ritual of atonement in the Temple. In the Ashkenazi rite there are three prostrations, one for each prayer uttered by the High Priest. In the Sephardi rite there is an additional prostration for the High Priest's announcement "A sin-offering for the Lord." Another difference between the Ashkenazi and Sephardi rites is that the former only relates the High Priest's countings in the Holy of Holies, whereas the latter adds two more which the High Priest counted as he stood in the outer sanctuary (*heikhal*) and sprinkled the blood on the curtain dividing the outer and inner sanctuaries.

A New Year greeting card depicting the *ḥazzan* prostrating himself, helped by one of the congregants.

The Reform movement, consistent with its rejection of the sacrificial cult, confines the ritual to the High Priest's confession, recited in Hebrew and in the vernacular. There is also no prostration, but instead prayers have been added emphasizing the moral duties to which Israel has to consecrate itself in order to bring about the kingdom of God on earth.

In the Conservative ritual, most parts of the traditional Hebrew *Avodah* service are retained, but, instead of translating them into English, new meditations and prayers of contemporary relevance are inserted as well as modern interpretations of the symbolism of the ancient Temple sacrificial service.

The description of the Temple service is followed by a beau-

A page from a 15th century handwritten prayer book from Fez, Morocco. It contains an introduction (*reshut*) to the *Avodah* service.

tiful *piyyut* describing, with intense nostalgia, the appearance of the High Priest as he successfully made his exit from the sanctuary. This is an adaptation from Ben Sira and introduces the *piyyutim* which describe the misfortunes of Israel now that there is no Temple or Temple service. Outstanding among these is a *piyyut* which relates the death of the "Ten Martyrs", among them Rabbi Ishmael, the High Priest, Rabbi Simeon ben Gamaliel and Rabbi Akiva. The Roman procurator is shown as searching for an excuse to kill the sages of Israel. He summons them and in seeming innocence puts to them a point in law: what punishment is due a kidnapper who sells his victim, a fellow Jew. The sages answer that his punishment is death. Thereupon the procurator informs them that Joseph's ten brothers were never punished and they, the most worthy representatives of their people, must atone for their sin. The sages wish to know if their fate is justified and turn to Rabbi Ishmael, who utters the Ineffable Name and receives the answer from heaven that their fate has been sealed by inscrutable Divine ordinance.

This moving description is poetic and not historical for these martyrs did not die at the same time. Rabbi Simeon ben Gamaliel, for instance, died at the time of the destruction of the Temple whereas Rabbi Akiva died in the aftermath of the Bar Kokhba revolt. Another of the martyrs, Judah ben Bava, is reported elsewhere to have been killed in completely different circumstances, when he illegally ordained five rabbis. A different version of the *piyyut* is recited on Tishah be-Av and still others are known to exist. The central idea of relating the death of martyrs during the Yom Kippur prayers has been enlarged by the Conservative rite which includes the recital of the death of Jewish martyrs during the Holocaust. Noteworthy is the description of the ninety-six Beth Jacob girls in Warsaw, who committed suicide in order to escape being taken to the German

Hanina ben Tradyon, one of the Ten Martyrs, being burnt at the stake.
From the *menorah* at the *Knesset* building by Benno Elkan.

brothels. There is also a poem by Frantisek Bass which describes the death of 155,000 Jewish children in Theresienstadt.

At the close of the day, following the afternoon *Minḥah* service, as the sun reaches treetop height, the *Ne'ilah* service is recited. This is the concluding service of the Day of Atonement and ends the day on a note of confidence.

Ne'ilah means "closing"; the full name of the *Ne'ilah* service is *Ne'ilat ha-Shearim,* the closing of the gates; but the sages differed as to which gates were closed: the daily closing of the Temple gates at sunset, or the closing of the heavenly gates. It is the latter meaning that is associated with *Ne'ilah* on Yom Kippur and it is this thought which gives the *Ne'ilah* service its poignancy. For this reason the ark of the Torah scrolls is kept open throughout the reader's repetition of the *Amidah* until the conclusion of the service.

Ne'ilah

Yom Kippur is the only time in the year that a fifth *Amidah* is added to the normal number of *amidot.* In the Second Temple period the *Ne'ilah* prayer was recited on all public fast days, and also by the lay and priestly "divisions" who accompanied the sacrificial services with prayers. Later, however, *Ne'ilah* was limited to Yom Kippur. As this is the concluding service, it is also the one that evokes the greatest fervor. It consists of introductionary prayers including *Ashrei* (Psalm 145), followed by the *Amidah* with the regular three opening and three closing benedictions of the statutory *amidot* and a specific central benediction. It, too, includes the short confession, but the *Al-Ḥet* is omitted. The prayers recapitulate the doctrine that God eagerly forgives the truly penitent. Since, according to rabbinic tradition, a man's fate is not sealed until the end of Yom Kippur, the prayer to "inscribe" is changed in the *Ne'ilah* service to "seal." The reader's repetition of the *Amidah* includes *piyyutim* and *seliḥot* with a frequent recital of the 13 divine attributes of

Illuminated page of the *Ne'ilah* service from the *Leipzig Maḥzor,* c. 1320.
The form of a gate is particularly fitting since the text is, "Open the gate
for us (i.e., our prayers) . . ."(above). Belt and buckle for *kitel* used on
the High Holy Days and Passover *seder* night. On the center panel is engraved the verse, "For on this day shall atonement be made for you. . .
(Leviticus 16:30) and underneath "Lublin" (Poland) is "Elul, 1821".
To the left is a goat used for atonement (opposite).

mercy. In many communities the priestly blessing, omitted in the *Minḥah* service, is recited during *Ne'ilah*. The service closes with *Avinu Malkenu* which in many communities is this time read out verse by verse. Then the first verse of *Shema*, "Hear O Israel, The Lord is our God, The Lord is One", is recited once; the verse, "Blessed be His glorious sovereign Name for ever and ever", three times and, "The Lord, He is God" repeated seven times. The number seven is an allusion to the seven firmaments through which the prayers pass to reach God. At the conclusion, *Kaddish*

Rabbi Shlomo Goren holding a Torah Scroll and blowing the *shofar* at the Western Wall immediately after the liberation of Jerusalem in 1967.

is recited by the *ḥazzan* and the *shofar* is blown. The custom of the *shofar* varies. In most Ashkenazi communities a single blast is sounded but some others blow *teki'ah shevarim teru'ah teki'ah.* In some communities the *shofar* is blown before *Kaddish,* in others after *Kaddish,* while others blow the *shofar* in the middle of *Kaddish.* In contrast to *Rosh Ha-Shanah* the *shofar* is blown on Yom Kippur even if it is a Sabbath, because it is already night, although *Havdalah* has not yet been recited.

Various reasons are given for blowing the *shofar.* It is a reminder of the *yovel* (the Jubilee year), when all property returned to its original owners, and all Jewish slaves were set free. This was announced by the blowing of the *shofar* on Yom Kippur. It is also an allusion to the verse, "The Lord is gone up with the blowing of the horn . . .". When God concluded the Sinai visitation and "went up" from the mount, the blast of the horn was heard, and signified the termination of God's presence on the mountain.

In Jerusalem it was customary to blow the *shofar* at the Western Wall. Following the Arab riots of 1929 the British mandatory authorities set up a committee of inquiry, followed by an international committee, which decided that although the Jews had uncontested right to worship at the wall, they were not to blow the *shofar* there. The Jews regarded this ruling as a searing humiliation and every year nationalist youth would make it a point of honor to blow the *shofar* at the wall at the termination of Yom Kippur, despite the danger from the Arabs, and the intervention of the British police. Many of these youths were arrested and imprisoned. Immediately following the capture of the Old City of Jerusalem in 1967, Rabbi Goren — at the time the Chief Chaplain of the Israel Defense Forces, at present Chief Rabbi of Israel — blew the *shofar* at the Western Wall as a symbol of its redemption.

After the service people wish each other, "The Next year in (rebuilt) Jerusalem." Only twice a year is this wish expressed. Once at the termination of the *Haggadah* on Pesaḥ night and once on Yom Kippur. This is in accordance with the difference of opinion between Rabbi Eliezer and Rabbi Joshua as to whether the Messiah will come to redeem Israel in Nisan or in Tishrei.

Moses receiving the Tablets of the Law, from *Amsterdam Minhagim Book*, 1662.

Halakhah and Custom

In the Bible, Yom Kippur is described as *Shabbat Shabbaton*, a Sabbath of Sabbaths. It is a Sabbath, and all the commandments of the Sabbath apply also to Yom Kippur. But it transcends the Sabbath in sanctity because of the sacrificial service and by virtue of its ultimate purpose. It also differs from the Sabbath in the five forms of self-denial practiced on Yom Kippur, as part of the repentance ritual. This self-denial, or "afflictions", affecting the basic functions of the human body, make Yom Kippur even more of a day of rest than the regular Sabbath.

A Sabbath of Sabbaths

100

Yom Kippur is referred to four times in the Pentateuch, three
times in Leviticus and once in Numbers. Chapter 16 in Leviticus,
which is the Torah reading for Yom Kippur morning (see
page 77), describes the sacrificial service on the Day of Atonement. Yom Kippur is mentioned again in the list of festivals and
a third time in connection with the Jubilee year. In Numbers, the
sacrifices of the day are listed. In each instance, except in the
reference to the Jubilee year, the Bible stressed the commandment that a person must "afflict" himself. Moreover, a transgression of this command involves the punishment of heavenly
extirpation *(karet)*. The commandment to afflict oneself is
directly related to the atonement which is granted on Yom
Kippur. Despite the great importance of the command, which is
shown both by the severe punishment entailed for transgression as
well as its clear connection with the very essence of Yom Kippur,
the Bible does not elaborate on the form which the "affliction"
is to take. The sages interpreted the "affliction" to apply to five
forms of self-denial: eating and drinking, washing and bathing,
anointing, cohabitation and wearing leather shoes or sandals. The
punishment of extirpation is applied only to eating and drinking.
Eating is defined as swallowing something bigger than a date. In
most halakhic laws touching on quantities of food, the size of an
olive serves as the criterion. On Yom Kippur the point in question is the measure of satisfaction and the sages argued that food
the size of an olive would not satisfy the appetite, whereas the
size of a date would alleviate the "affliction" suffered. By eating
the equivalent of a date a person becomes liable to extirpation,
but the prohibition of eating food on Yom Kippur applies to any
quantity, however small. If fasting involves danger to life, the
halakhah clearly permits a person to eat. Even should the patient
claim that he can fast, as long as the doctor thinks that he should
eat, he must eat. If, however, the patient himself feels that he

must eat then even should a hundred doctors say he can fast, he is nevertheless permitted to eat. Once, during a cholera plague, when it was thought to be dangerous to fast as it would weaken the body's resistance, Rabbi Israel Salanter, an important rabbi in Russia in the 19th century and the founder of the Musar (Ethics) movement, ordered the congregation to eat and himself ate in their presence as an example. If possible, a person who has to eat on Yom Kippur should do so in a series of very small quantities, smaller than the size of a date, pausing between each, so that within a nine-minute period, he will not have eaten more than the equivalent of three eggs. This does not apply to children who are encouraged to eat on Yom Kippur and who can be fed by grown-ups. Only from the age of nine or ten upwards should they be taught gradually to fast, usually by forgoing their breakfast for an hour or two. A girl at the age of twelve and a boy at the age of thirteen are considered old enough to undertake all the commandments, and this includes fasting. A mother, within three days of giving birth, is not allowed to fast. From three to seven days after birth she can eat if she feels it is necessary.

Those who have to eat on Yom Kippur do not recite *Kiddush* (although one halakhic authority does require it), but they do include the special festival addition, *Ya'ale ve-Yavo*, in the Grace after Meals because Yom Kippur is a festival.

Fasting appears frequently in the Bible as a sign of repentance. The people of Nineveh fasted on hearing Jonah's message. So did Esther and the Jews for three days before she risked her life by going, uninvited, to see King Ahasuerus. Fasting also served the purpose of enhancing the spiritual in man. By restraining the material requirements of the body, the mind can focus more clearly on the spiritual. A fast also reduces the fat content of the body which is reckoned as if he had brought a sacrifice, the fat of which is offered on the altar of God.

102

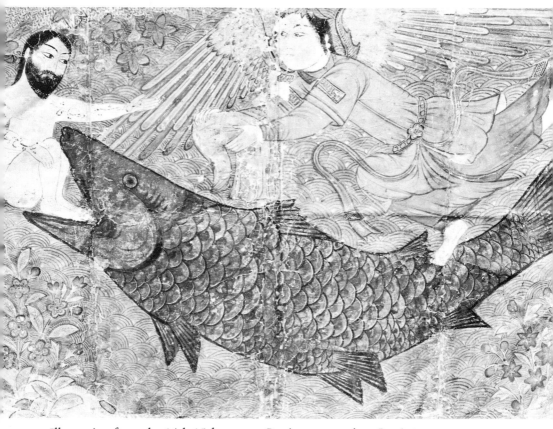

Illustration from the 14th-15th century Persian manuscript, *Jami at-Tawarikh* by Rashid ad-Din, showing Jonah being cast up by the whale.

Washing and bathing is prohibited only when it causes gratification or comfort. For this reason a person does not wash his face or hands on Yom Kippur. In the morning, on getting up, or before prayers the fingers are washed up to the knuckles. Anointing, nowadays, applies mainly to face and hand creams. In ancient times anointing the body with olive oil was a regular habit, especially after bathing. The prohibition of cohabitation caused two divergent customs. One was to leave lighted candles in the bedroom; the other was not to light lamps at all in order that a person should not see his wife and be tempted. Only shoes or sandals of leather are prohibited whether the top or the sole is of leather, but shoes made of cloth, rubber, plastic or wood are permitted.

Kiddush Levanah ("Blessing the Moon"), etching by Lionel S. Reiss.

Yom Kippur is the only festival which is not celebrated for a second day in the Diaspora. It would have been too difficult to fast for two whole days, although certain rabbis in the past did do so, sometimes with fatal consequences.

At the termination of the meal before Yom Kippur the table is cleared and a clean white cloth spread on it in honor of the festival. Yom Kippur is a time of repentance and soul-searching. At the same time there is an atmosphere of confidence that man's repentance will be accepted, and, like Rosh Ha-Shanah, so too, Yom Kippur is a festival. The mistress of the house lights candles reciting the blessing for Yom Kippur and the *She-heḥeyanu* benediction. It is customary to light a *Yahrzeit*-light for one's deceased parents on those days when *Yizkor* is recited. On Yom Kippur many people light an additional *Yahrzeit*-light in the synagogue. As on Rosh Ha-Shanah, the *kitel* is worn in the synagogue. In England, in certain communities, top hats and tails are worn for the *Kol Nidrei* Service. It is also customary to wear the *tallit* (prayer shawl) in the evening. This is put on immediately on entry into the synagogue so that the blessing may be recited before nightfall. In most synagogues, the ark and the central *bimah* are also covered with white so as to enhance the atmosphere of purity. The very devout remain in the synagogue all night reciting psalms. During the day it is customary in many congregations to pass round a spice box over which the blessing for spices is recited. This is in accordance with the rabbinic view that a hundred benedictions should be recited daily. On Yom Kippur when the *Amidah* contains only seven benedictions instead of the normal nineteen, and no blessings for meals are recited, the number of benedictions is greatly restricted.

It is an ancient custom to recite the blessing over the new moon every month. In the month of Tishrei this is delayed until the night following Yom Kippur, when it is said by the congregation immediately after the service, before breaking the fast. The *Havdalah* after Yom Kippur is similar to that after the Sabbath but with two differences. First, the benediction over spices is omitted. According to rabbinic tradition, the Jew receives an extra soul on the Sabbath which leaves him at its termination. He therefore sniffs the pleasant fragrance of the spices at the outgoing of the Sabbath in order to revive him as the extra soul leaves. On Yom Kippur there is no extra soul because of the affliction one suffers from fasting. The second difference is that after the Sabbath a benediction is recited over a newly-lit light because, on that night, Adam took two stones, rubbed them together and created fire. This reason does not apply to Yom Kippur, however, it is forbidden on Yom Kippur to light a fire, a prohibition which is lifted when the day terminates. The benediction signifies the permissibility of using fire again, and thus,

Havdalah woodcut from *Venice Minhagim Book*, 1601(?). The benediction over the light is being recited.

only a light which has burned for the whole of Yom Kippur is used for the benediction.

The night following Yom Kippur is considered a minor festival. It is considered commendable to eat and drink. The Midrash relates that at the close of Yom Kippur a heavenly voice used to be heard telling the people to go home and eat, to drink and be merry because God had accepted their prayers. The High Priest, too, used to make a feast for his friends and for the people, after Yom Kippur in thanksgiving for successfully concluding the daily service. In order to begin the new period with the performance of a biblical commandment, it is customary to begin building the *Sukkah* that very same night.

5.   DAYS OF AWE

The High Holy Days are remarkable for the impact they make on all who have experienced them to the full — an impression that sometimes remains for a lifetime. The Days of Awe seem to embody the whole spirit of Judaism. Thus for the religious Jew they become the climax of the year, for the non-religious they become a last link with tradition, while for the anti-religious the Days of Awe become the symbol against which they rebel. In each case the Days of Awe are associated with the very essence of Judaism. Agnon, in the introduction to his book *Days of Awe,* recounts the impression made on him at the age of four by attendance at the synagogue, and this impression was reinforced in later life. Like many others, he attempts to analyze the cause of this impression. Is it the prayers of the High Holy Days, or the particular tunes? Is it the ecstatic recital of the reader, or the pervading tone of common purpose? For Agnon it was above all the atmosphere of sanctity, as the congregation stood enwrapped in prayer shawls, engrossed in prayer.   107

The *Kol Nidrei* service in a German synagogue.

Agnon's description is true not only of East European Jewry but of many congregations the world over. The synagogue service on the High Holy Days has always been considered vital. Outlying Jewish settlements take extreme measures to ensure having at least a *minyan* (ten congregants) for the service. On the other hand, more populous communities frequently hold "overflow" services as the synagogue is not big enough for all the participants

108

crowding the building on the High Holy Days. Indeed, a charac-
teristic feature of contemporary synagogue architecture is the
"expanding synagogue." Considerable stress is always laid on
procuring a suitable *hazzan* to lead the services, especially the
climactic *musaf* service. Certain communities insist on an ac-
complished musical rendition; others closely examine the saint-
liness of the *hazzan's* character. In many cities today the services
are advertized on billboards and in the newspapers, which give
prominence to the name of the *hazzan* who will lead the service.

It is perhaps surprising how little the High Holy Days have
changed in the course of 2,000 years. As is shown by the passage
from Philo (see page 62), they have remained essentially the
same since the days of the Second Temple — excepting, of
course, the central ceremony in the Temple, especially that on
Yom Kippur, when the High Priest entered the inner sanctuary,
the only time during the year that this was allowed. Originally
the Holy of Holies contained only the ark with the tablets of
stone and the Torah. In the Second Temple the room remained
completely empty (much to the astonishment of Pompey, the
Roman general, who in 63 b.c.e. forced his way into the inner
sanctuary). When the High Priest entered the Holy of Holies on
the Day of Atonement he was completely alone, and as he was
the representative of the Jewish people, this was understood as a
direct confrontation, once a year, of the people with God. The
rabbis averred that even the angles were denied access to this
encounter.

The sanctity of that moment of confrontation has been
preserved in the synagogue service, except that since the destruction of the Temple it cannot take place through a representative.
Everyone is expected to participate, even those who normally
have little contact with Judaism or the community. This involve-
ment is illustrated by the hasidic tale of a young shepherd's boy

109

who could not read or speak Hebrew. He came to the synagogue with his flute in his pocket and listened to the service in growing wonder. He was seized with an ever-growing desire to participate, but owing to his ignorance did not know how. Finally, as the congregation reached the *Ne'ilah* prayers, he could no longer contain his desperate desire to express himself and, taking the flute out of his pocket, blew a long piercing blast. Seeing the consternation he had caused, the lad fled back to his fields. At the conclusion of the service the Ba'al Shem Tov stated that it was the shepherd boy who had opened the gates of heaven, allowing the prayers of the congregation to ascend, because his motives had been of the purest, to pray directly to God.

This anti-formalism and emphasis on basic morals is not confined to Ḥasidism. It finds expression in Peretz's story of the rabbi who, instead of going to *seliḥot* in the early morning, would secretly help the poor and aged while his congregation prayed. It is even related of the saintly Rabbi Israel Salanter that once he did not come to *Kol Nidrei* He was eventually found returning a stray cow to its non-Jewish owner. Thus Rabbi Israel Salanter absented himself from the most important evening service of the year in order to return the lost property of a gentile. These tales stress the purity of intention and the consideration for others which are prerequisite to the service of God. The High Holy Days should be the peak of man's spiritual experience during the year, which must include the love for one's fellow. This, Hillel stated, is the basic tenet of Judaism.

The pivotal concept of the High Holy Days was perhaps best summed up by one of Israel's greatest sages, Rabbi Akiva: "Happy is your lot, O Israel! Before whom do you purify yourself, and who purifies you? Your Father in Heaven." Before Israel can seek divine purification it must first find its own purification — and that in the field of interpersonal relationships.

110

"Yom Kippur in the Country" by Alphonse Levy.

Adar, twelfth month of the Jewish year (February-March).

Amidah, main prayer recited at all regular services, said standing and in silence

Ashkenazi (pl. Ashkenazim), German or West-, Central-, or East European Jew(s), as contrasted with Sephardim.

Avodah, the Temple ritual performed by the High Priest on the Day of Atonement, and applied to that day's Musaf liturgy.

Elul, sixth month of the Jewish year (August-September).

Erev, the evening; often used to denote the day preceeding the Sabbath or festival.

Etrog, citron; used on Sukkot as a ritual object.

Habad, hasidic movement whose leader is the Rabbi of Lubavich.

Haftarah, designation of the portion from the prophetical books of the Bible recited in the synagogue after the Pentateuchal reading.

Haggadah, ritual recited in the home on Passover eve.

Halakhah, an accepted decision in rabbinic law.

Hasidism, religious movement which adopted a liturgical rite based on changes made by Isaac Luria (1534-72).

Havdalah, ceremony marking the end of the Sabbath or festival.

Hazzan, reader, cantor.

Hoshanah Rabbah, the seventh day of the Sukkot festival.

Kaddish, liturgical prayer in Aramaic.

Kedushah, addition to the third benediction in the reader's repetition of the *Amidah.*

Kiddush, prayer of sanctification, recited over wine on Sabbaths and festivals.

Kitel, white garment worn as a sign of purity or as an evocation of death on solemn occasions.

Lulav, palm branch; used on Sukkot as a ritual object.

Maftir, the concluding portion of the Pentateuchal portion on Sabbaths and festivals.

Midrash, rabbinic compilation interpreting scriptures.

Minhah, afternoon prayer.

Musaf, additional prayer on Sabbaths, festivals and New Moon.

Ne'ilah, concluding prayer on the Day of Atonement.

Nisan, first month of the Jewish year (March-April)

Paytan, composer of liturgical poems.

Pesah, Passover.

Pilgrim Festivals, the three festivals, Passover, Shavuot, and Sukkot.

Piyyut, Hebrew liturgical composition.

Rosh Ḥodesh, semi-festival; first day (or two) of the lunar month.

Sanhedrin, the assembly of ordained scholars which functioned as a supreme court. It originally convened in a special building in the Temple compound.

Seliḥot, penitential prayer.

Sephardi (pl. Sephardim), Jew(s) of Spain and Portugal and their descendants, wherever resident; often loosely used for Oriental Jews when contrasted with Ashkenazi.

Shaḥarit, morning service.

Shavuot, Pentecost, Feast of Weeks.

She-heḥeyanu, benediction, praising the Almighty for having sustained us.

Shemini Aẓeret, a festival completing the Sukkot festival.

Shemittah, Sabbatical year.

Shevat, eleventh month of the Jewish year (January-February).

Shofar, horn; usually a ram's horn.

Sukkot, (festival of) Tabernacles.

Tallit, prayer shawl.

Tishrei, seventh month of the Jewish year (September-October).

Yizkor, memorial prayer.

Yom Tov, festival day.

Yovel, Jubilee year.

ABBREVIATIONS OF SOURCES

BIBLE

Gen.	— Genesis	Is.	— Isaiah	Song.	— Song of Songs
Ex.	— Exodus	Jer.	— Jeremiah	Ecc.	— Ecclesiastes
Lev.	— Leviticus	Ezek.	— Ezekiel	Esth.	— Esther
Num.	— Numbers	Hos.	— Hosea	Ez.	— Ezra
Deut.	— Deuteronomy	Zeph.	— Zephaniah	Neh.	— Nehemiah
		Ps.	— Psalms	Macc.	— Maccabees

TALMUD[1]

TJ	— Jerusalem Talmud[2]			San.	— *Sanhedrin*
Ar.	— *Arakhin*	Kid.	— *Kiddushin*	Shav.	— *Shavuot*
Git.	— *Gittin*	Meg.	— *Megillah*	Ta'an.	— *Ta'anit*
Ker.	— *Keritot*	R.H.	— *Rosh Ha-Shanah*	Tam.	— *Tamid*

LATER AUTHORITIES

Yad — Maimonides, *Yad Ḥazakah*
Sh. Ar., OH — *Shulḥan Arukh, Oraḥ Hayyim*

[1] References to the Mishnah are in the form Git. 10:6 (i.e., *Tractate Gittin,* chapter 10, Mishnah 6); references to the Gemara are in the form Git. 64a (i.e., *Tractate Gittin,* page 64, first side).

[2] Otherwise all Talmud references are to the Babylonian Talmud.

116

117

Encyclopedia Judaica, Jerusalem, 1972, under: *Avodah, Al-Het, Ashamnu, Avinu Malkenu,* Day of Atonement, *Kapparot, Kol Nidrei,* Liturgy, *Ne'ilah, Rosh Ha-Shanah, Shofar,* Ten Days of Penitence, *U-Netanneh Tokef*

Agnon, S.Y., *Days of Awe,* New York, 1965.
Gaster, T.H., *Festivals of the Jewish Year,* New York, 1955.
Goodman, P., *Rosh Hashanah Anthology,* Philadelphia, 1970.
Jacobs, Louis, *A Guide to Rosh Ha-Shanah,* London, 1959.
————— , *A Guide to Yom Kippur,* London, 1957.
Lehrman, S.M., *The Solemn Festivals,* Torah Va'avodah Library (Festival Series 6), London, 1943.
Munk, E., *The World of Prayer,* vol 2, New York, 1954.

119

En-Harod, Mishkan la-Ommanut, facing p. 1
Tel Aviv, Israel Government Press Office, p. 2,21,49,67,85,98
A. Yaari, *Hebrew Printers' Marks,* Jerusalem, 1943, p. 4
Cecil Roth Collection, p. 7,31,63,65,68,78,111
Amsterdam, Stedelijk Museum, p. 8
Dresden, Sächsische Landesbibliothek, p. 10
Jerusalem, Israel Museum, p. 11,17,23,35,52,53,83,104; color: pl. 1,2 (bottom),
   3 (top), 4, 6 (bottom)
Jerusalem, Jewish National and University Library, p. 14,47,87,100; color: pl. 5
B. Chagall, *Burning Lights,* New York, 1946, p.22
Photo Kluger, Tel Aviv, p. 24
New York, Jewish Theological Seminary, p. 26,58,76
Morris U. Schappes, *The Jews in the United States,* New York, 1953, p. 27
Leipzig, University Library, p. 30, 96; color: pl. 3 (bottom)
Paris, Bibliotheque nationale, p. 38,92
Amsterdam, Nederlands-Israelietische Hoofdsynagoge, p. 40
New York, Metropolitan Museum of Art, p. 43,103
Baltimore, Md., Walters Art Gallery, p. 44
G. Liebe, *Das Judentum in der deutschen Vergangenheit,* Leipzig, 1903, p. 48
Mme. D. Kirszenbaum, Paris, p. 50
Moritz Oppenheim, *Bilder aus dem altjüdischen Familienleben,* 1865, p. 55
Jerusalem, Sir Isaac and Lady Wolfson Museum, p. 56, 97; color: pl. 6 (top)
Atlas of Israel, Jerusalem, 1970, p. 61
Hebrew-Latin Mishnah, Amsterdam, 1700-04, p. 62
A.Z. Idelsohn, *Melodien 8,* 1932, p. 71
U.S. Signal Corps Photo, p. 73
Bene-Berak, Wallersteiner Collection, p. 75
Kirschner, *Jüdisches Ceremoniel,* Nurenberg, 1734, p. 80, 81
Israel Foreign Office, p. 82
Cleveland, Ohio, Joseph B. Horowitz Collection, p. 84
Budapest, Hungarian Academy of Science, p. 89
Itzhak Amit, Kibbutz Zorah, p. 94
Oxford, Bodleian Library, p. 106
B. Picart, *Ceremonies et coutumes religieuses,* Amsterdam, 1723, p. 108
New York, Jewish Museum, color: pl. 2 (top)
Photo Werner Braun, Jerusalem, color: pl. 7,8

Cover: "Jews at Prayer on the Day of Atonement" by Maurycy Gottlieb, oil, 1878.
   The Tel Aviv Museum